My Manette—Photographs and Little Stories
1941-1951

Written and Illustrated
© 2014—DeAnna K. Johnson Kauzlaric Kieffer
Bremerton, Washington USA
All rights reserved.

Contact and Order Information:
DeAnna K. Kauzlaric Kieffer at *mymanette@wavecable.com*
Website: *www.deannajkk.info*

Carlyn Smueles, Editor

Acknowledgement

Thanks to the family members, friends, neighbors and classmates who are part of *My Manette*. In spirit, they are there today. I remember and honor them by believing the best of the community I knew now beats in new hearts and lives with the best intentions of Manette residents today.

Front Cover Photograph

Manette Grade School 1945—Miss Lottie Bell's First Grade Class

Our class photo was not distributed at the time because of the indelicate poses of some of the young ladies in the first row. This decision was made by school authorities. Sixty-two years later, Sandra Fisher Schmidt (sixth from left in front row) shared this rare photo at a pre-50th high school reunion party. I am in the second row, third from the right.

Thank you Sandi.

Back Cover Photograph by Jan Williams

ISBN-13: **978-1501081804**
ISBN-10: **1501081802**

Dedicated to my sister and brother

Jacquolyn Jean Johnson Smalley
1932-2007

Montgomery Dean Johnson
1933-2000

Note:

Some of these little stories may not be suitable for tender sensibilities.

Also, cousin Marjorie Johnson was called Margie as a child but preferred Marj as an adult.

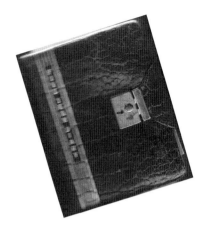

No Apologies

When Aunt Kay and Uncle Bill Higgin gave me my first diary, they introduced me to a new friend. I had secretly wanted one for some time. My entries began on New Year's Day 1949 and mention my parent's visit to Tacoma, going to a movie with a neighbor kid Bobby Isaacson, and how big my rabbit had grown. These are the exciting entries and almost as scintillating as the entry which apologizes to my "dear diary" because I had temporarily lost its/my key.

Overall, they are heartfelt entries spilling onto the pages marked with childish enthusiasm and little regard for the niceties of polite sentence structure—or correct spelling. Consequently, they are funny and awful at the same time. I wrote these little stories over a period of ten years. While putting this collection together, I took clues from my diary entries and used the terminology of the time and expressions common to my contemporaries. Whether that era's frame of mind is more or less sensitive than today's critic, I'll leave for others to decide.

I reviewed over 400 photographs in my Manette collection for inclusion in *My Manette*. Most were taken by Uncle Aubrey Monson or my mother. I tried to include those that show something of the Manette landscape of the time, even though the original intent was simply to capture images of immediate family, relatives and friends. One thing the photographs seem to have in common: the family dogs are in almost every one of them.

1942—Mother and Dad (Ferne and George Johnson) and myself with our dog Pat, not long after we moved to Manette. We are standing on the Monson dock of my aunt and uncle's duplex home at 101 Shore Drive, also known, at the time, as the "front yard" of their place.

1943—A Sunday picnic on the Monson duplex deck. My dad and I are on the bench and my mother is to his left. With us are some of Uncle Aubrey's Monson relatives from the Tacoma area, plus a visiting sailor or two. Note the boats moored on the north side of the dock (upper left of the photo). Uncle Aubrey operated the Manette Boat Rental business during this time.

The Monson dock is now part of the Boatshed Restaurant in Manette.

1943-Aubrey made the roll-up awning for the west facing windows of the duplex.

Note the bottles on the right by the end of the plank fencing—no doubt remnants of Monson hospitality.

THE BUS STOP

Thoughts—ideas—memories are not convenient. Some of the best of them occur at inopportune times, even when we are young. It wouldn't be true to say that life passed before my eyes at the age of three but clearly I *saw* something that day at the bus stop.

Not all bus stops in Manette were on hills, but those on the west side of East 11th Street certainly were. From our home on East 11th and Shore Drive, my mom and I walked up the sidewalk and waited almost directly across the street from the barber shop that was on the corner at Perry Avenue. I may have been wearing one of my favorite bonnets. I recall the sky was bright as I held her hand waiting for the bus to take us across the bridge to Bremerton.

Simply put, I "saw" my mind. The colors and the sensation were over quickly. What did remain was the idea that I saw something I shouldn't see, just yet. The memory of that singular and closely spiritual moment is still vivid. I have tried to revisit the picture and describe it to others, but have failed. It was something like Sir Arthur Sullivan's *The Lost*

Chord—a fleeting, unforgettable moment. What did remain was how I would see the world afterward. And, it made me think. It made me think old.

Kids are simply adults with limitations. As if it weren't enough to start out with a wobbly head and eyes that don't focus. Add to this a lack of experience upon which lessons can be attached. We go through childhood constantly coping and adjusting. We do things to gain know-how. We get in trouble just to find out what will happen next. We can debate whether it's a good idea or not, while all around us stuff continues to happen.

Some of the things I remember about growing up in Manette in the 1940-50s are presented here: a random collection of stories without the benefit of adult supervision. My memories of the events and characters (including my mother) are mature enough for the time. If this "maturity" affected my social life, then that was a burden I had to bear. I wasn't typical, but no kid is. And now, after years of experience, I know most excuses about being "different" have more to do with what's inside than outside. I could guess at other reasons, like being taller, talking too much, or imitating a lack-talent English actor when I was 12, but I suspect it is more a matter of just being me.

These little stories do not pretend to be a comprehensive history of Manette with dutiful research, solid facts and genealogies complete with pie charts. No, they are wayward vignettes influenced by the locale—the beach, the bridge, the ferries and other things of that time. They are pinpoint observations and impressions about the people I thought I knew and the very human situations that I experienced in my Manette neighborhood.

Kids are pint-size *adults* but no one knows it, yet.

1942—My third birthday with "must have" guests. I don't recall exactly who was who. I do recognize (front row l-r) Cousin Margie, unknown, myself (with balloon), and unknown.
(second row) Virginia and Janice Ottevaere, brother Monty and unknown boy on his left,
(third row) sister Jackie and Barbara Ward on her left. With us are some big neighborhood kids who probably came just for the cake.
In my baby book, my mother listed other guests as Ralph Patan and Charles, Ernest and Larry Elliott.

Above—Early 1940s—A couple enjoys a boat ride in the *Mary Glenn* in this photograph taken by Uncle Aubrey from his "front yard" dock of the Monson duplex on Shore Drive. Note the girder system on the original Manette Bridge that spans the columns to the center. The girders were easily accessed from the east side above the beach.

MY MANETTE

If there was a beginning of My Manette it would be with Aunt Velma and Uncle Aubrey. She was my mother's only sister. M. Velma Monson and Aubrey Gerald Monson had been living in Tacoma and later in Bremerton before my folks moved our family to Bremerton in 1941.

A congenial couple, Velma and Aubrey shared many interests. Both were talented visionaries who used lots of elbow grease to bring their ideas to reality. They met in Scottsbluff, Nebraska where they worked at a shoe store. In 1933, Velma was still in high school and a part-time clerk, but she married Aubrey on New Year's Eve after a 10-day courtship.

Aubrey was from Wisconsin but graduated high school in Ft. Lauderdale, Florida. He attended an art institute in Madison, Wisconsin. and worked as a commercial display/designer and salesman. He was a fine illustrator and an expert at hand lettering. His credentials included a degree in cinematography so a camera was rarely far away. He delighted in life's smaller moments. Many of his photographs and movies reflect this. A collection of slides, photographs and films taken in the Tacoma area is at the Tacoma Historical Museum.

Velma and Aubrey welcomed family and friends into their world with enthusiasm. During World War II, their friends included many servicemen stationed in Bremerton. They had no children but doted on a long succession of black Labrador dogs, all of which were named Pepper.

Sometime in her eighties, Velma wrote an account of those early years for the first Manette history book. She hoped it might accompany some of the photographs she offered. Because of constraint of space in the history book, she kept it brief; so her narrative doesn't contain many of the details she might have otherwise included. A photograph of Aubrey with one of the boats from their boat rental business, relocated to Shore Drive from Washington Beach, was the only item used. Her account follows on the next page.

Above—1942 Velma enjoys a sunny day on the beach.
Below—1943 Aubrey after a swim in Dyes Inlet from the Monson dock.

Manette Days

by M. Velma Monson Dopheide

Invasion Prompts Move to Bremerton

In 1937, my husband Aubrey Gerald Monson and I were living in Billings, Montana. We had visited and lived in Tacoma a few years earlier because Aubrey had an aunt, uncle and cousins in the area. When Germany invaded Poland in September of 1939, we came back to the Northwest. He thought the area would have increased job opportunities if the United States became involved in the conflict. For a brief time we lived in Tacoma, but we moved to Bremerton in January of 1940, on my 24th birthday.

Aubrey first worked at Travis and Yowell, a hardware store on Pacific Avenue. As with previous jobs, he did window display, advertising, and sales. We lived in a rented house on Washington Beach which was accessed by stairs from Washington Avenue. In March of that year, we started a boat rental business at that location. Aubrey commissioned and bought several classic boats from the Sulfur Spring boat works for the business.

My Family

My sister Ferne Johnson and her husband George moved to Bremerton from Nebraska with their three children in October of 1941. Initially, George was a baker at the Farmer's Market owned by Carl Swanson. He then went to work in Shop 02 in Puget Sound Naval Shipyard that involved work on the rail transports between Bremerton and regional fuel and munitions depots. My sister worked briefly at Keyport and later at Sears and Barr's Apparel in downtown Bremerton. When she re-entered civil service, it was as a practical nurse at Navy Hospital. Later, she transferred to the Supply Department and worked there until her retirement in 1963. Their first home was a few houses south of us on Shore Drive.

In August of 1944, they bought a house they had been renting on East 11th Street across from Etten Grocery, later known as *Roy and Glenn's Market* (Roy Etten and Glenn Jarstad). As part of the transaction, my sister and husband had to have the house relocated, so it was moved several blocks up the East 11th Street hill to the corner of Vandalia. About that time, Stan's Drive-Inn was built on 11th Street and Upper Shore Drive (next to the Market) and quickly became a favorite teen hangout.

We sold the Shore Drive property in 1947 to David Wheaton. He sold it to McCowan who established the namesake boat works there that was later owned and operated by Ansel Sawyer for many years before it became the location of the Boat Shed Restaurant.

Boat Rentals

In 1941, we purchased property at 101 Shore Drive in Manette from Oscar Hilstad. The property was formerly a coal dock and general store. It was where a passenger-vehicle ferry crossing operated prior to the construction of the first Manette Bridge in 1930. It was in disrepair. We cleared and tore down part of the dock, replaced posts and rebuilt the pier; then constructed a duplex on the north edge of the property. The remaining pier was our front porch. Friends Alex Ottevaere, business manager at *The Bremerton Sun*, his father, and Elton Dickens, advertising manager at the newspaper, helped us build the duplex. We reopened the boat rental business from the Shore Drive location in the fall and added a boat launch feature. The impact of World War II made it difficult to continue the business due to marine traffic restrictions and the shortage of parts needed for winch maintenance on the launch. Also, in 1942, Aubrey went to work as a machinist at Puget Sound Naval Shipyard, Shop 06 and the sail loft.

Later, Elton and his wife Helen lived in the other side of the duplex until he went into the Army Air Force. Elton was killed over Normandy, France on D-Day in June of 1944. A daughter, Lana Marie, was born to them after his death. Later, Helen married Clarence Monson, Aubrey's cousin, who was a school principal in Tacoma after the war. During the war, Clarence had seen action in the Pacific Theater and came back with health problems. They had a son Stephen about 1950.

WASHINGTON BEACH

217 Washington Avenue
Bremerton, Washington—1940

Aubrey worked at Travis and Yowell on Pacific Avenue, a hardware and general merchandise store, six days a week, They operated Monson's Boat Rental on the weekends.

A

B

C

F

A—Velma and Pepper in a Monson rental boat.

B—Aubrey and Velma with Pepper in their "front yard" Manette is across Dyes Inlet behind them.

C—Pepper in rowboat near shore. The upper buildings are on Washington Avenue.
Note the rental boats in the water on the left.

D—Uncle Fred and Aunt Dorothy Johnson (front right) and friends at a "boat picnic" at the Washington Beach property.

E—Aubrey on Washington Beach. Note the building in the background on the right. Port Orchard is across the water. This were several "dock buildings" in those earlier years.

F—Helen Dickens and Velma Monson on the Washington Beach "boardwalk" by their homes.

E

D

Manette Beach
101 Shore Drive
Bremerton, Washington—1943

With help of friends and colleagues, Velma and Aubrey made major renovations to the Shore Drive property in about two year's time.

Besides building the duplex, they moved their boat rental business to Shore Drive and renamed it Manette Boat Rentals.

Right—Real Estate agents on the Shore Drive property before my aunt and uncle bought it.
Below—A 1941 view of the Monson duplex from Upper Shore Drive after the grass was seeded.

Above—The duplex at 101 Shore Drive in Manette was the home of my Aunt Velma and Uncle Aubrey Monson between 1941 and 1947. Much of the timber and lumber that went into its construction were salvaged from the original dock, general store and "transportation center" that occupied the location previously. A small ferry and/or packet boat took vehicles and passengers back and forth to downtown Bremerton until the first Manette Bridge was built in 1930. Aunt Velma was unhappy that I enlarged and shared this photo with the Boat Shed Restaurant management because she didn't think her laundry hanging on the clothesline (mid-right) was very attractive.

1942—View of the pilings and dock south of the Monson duplex.

Another under-construction view of the Monson duplex "front yard" dock (now part of the dining space of the Boat Shed Restaurant) with the original Manette Bridge beyond. The main building of McCollum boat shed built in the 1950s was located on the SE corner of the property close to Shore Drive.

1943—View of the Monson duplex from Upper Shore Drive after the grass was seeded.

Downtown Bremerton is across Dyes Inlet.

LIFE ON THE DOCK

The Monson dock was the multi-purpose area for family meals, recreation and photographs.

1942

Top—1942 (l-r) Alex Ottevaere and Elton Dickens (both worked for the *Bremerton Sun*), unknown military man, Uncle Aubrey, and my dad, George Johnson.
Part of the general store and ferry service building is behind them on the right.

Right—1943 my mother, Ferne Johnson, with the first Manette Bridge behind her.

Bottom—1942 Brother Monty sitting in front of (l-r) my dad, Uncle Aubrey Monson, his cousin Clarence Monson, my mother, and Aubrey's cousin Robert Monson... and Pepper, of course.

1943 Sister Jackie and myself standing on the end of the diving board of the Monson duplex on a spring day.

Above—1942 Aubrey Monson's employee ID photo for Puget Naval Shipyard when he began work there as a machinist and in the sail loft. He was 35-years old.

Left—1940 Helen Dickens and Aunt Velma. Uncle Aubrey's may never have used these photos with an advertising theme of "sex sells" but they do capture some of the fun my aunt and uncle had with their rental business.

Below right—1940 Elton Dickens and Aubrey Monson with the male version of a "sexy sailor" who wants you to rent a boat.

Below left—1943- Pepper ignores the ferry Kalakala on one of his many boat rides.

18

Above—1940-1 A couple of the Monson rental boats moored in Dyes Inlet off Washington Beach before World War II began.

Left—1941 Unknown sailor standing on the Monson dock. The photograph looks south. A portion of Parker's Manette Lumber and dock can be seen behind him.

Below—1941 On the Monson dock (with the duplex under construction): unknown man, Elton Dickens, Helen Dickens and Aunt Velma Monson, Uncle Fred and Aunt Dorothy Johnson with their daughter Marjorie... and Pepper, of course.

1942—Posing with my doll shortly before my tonsillectomy at Dr. Jackson's office on Pacific Avenue—a same-day surgery. Dr. Jackson would later partner with Dr. Salmon and relocate as The Doctor's Clinic on Fifth Street in Bremerton.

Note the timber bulkhead between Shore Drive and Upper Shore Drive. Stairs to Upper Shore Drive were few and far between. Uncle Aubrey rebuilt the steps to the duplex and installed a better railing.

Above—The duplex is still under construction. The dock building on the north of the duplex was later removed.
Below—Snowstorm of 1942—Monty, Jackie and Uncle Aubrey wave at the camera on a snowy day in the yard of the Monson Shore Drive duplex. Pepper is waving, too—with his tail.

1943—Behind me is Oscar Etten's Super Market across the street on East 11th Street and Pitt Avenue. The market would later become Roy and Glen's Market after World War II ended.

Stan's Drive-In was the first business in the new building constructed next to the Market on the west (water) side.

Below—1943 Family picnic at the Monson Shore Drive duplex (back l-r) Lois and Ross Condley (dad's cousin and husband—stationed in Bremerton in the Navy), Grandmothers Myrtle Johnson and Travilla Clark, Aunt Mary K Johnson and Dean Rupard (middle) dad, mother, Aunt Velma (front) Monty, Bobby Dean Clark, Jackie, me and my cousin Carlyn Rupard, then a toddler.

Above—Dad, Bobby Dean and Aubrey at the same picnic.

Right—1943 with Oscar Etten's Super Market behind me (across East 11th Street).

Radio Waves

Like the other houses on Washington Beach in Bremerton, Uncle Fred and Aunt Dorothy Johnson's rental was built on pilings. From their front door, it was a steep climb up wooden steps with sporadic wooden handrails, to Washington Avenue where it intersected with Sixth Street. It was a built-in aerobic exercise program. The side areas were naturals for dirt sledding and filling shoes with rocks and mud.

My Aunt Velma and Uncle Aubrey's first house on the beach was only a few doors away. This is where they lived and first established Monson's Boat Rentals before they moved directly across the Port Washington Narrows to Shore Drive in Manette (East Bremerton).

From Manette on a clear day, it was easy to see if my cousin Margie was playing outside on the wraparound porch, a "deck" probably three feet wide with chicken wire strung in front of the railings. It was an ideal outside play spot with a grand view: the Manette Bridge, Mount Rainier; but, more importantly, ferries, boats, and the beach. From here, usually, Uncle Fred thought it was easier to row across the Narrows than walk the half mile up Washington Avenue and across the Manette Bridge.

Before WWII, Fred was a shoe salesman at the Buster Brown Shoe Store on Pacific Avenue, the trendiest shoe store for kids. Here there was easy access to a fluoroscope machine to view wiggly toes inside the sturdy brown oxfords preferred by parents. *Buster Brown* had other "rewards" for children, and always with a picture of Buster and his dog. Most important, Buster Brown sponsored the "Buster Brown Show," a half-hour Saturday morning radio program with plucky stories of daring do. Drawing upon the popularity of a cartoon strip by Richard Outcault, *Buster Brown* and his dog were an enticing advertising campaign to sell shoes. Their radio jingle, "I'm Buster Brown, I live in a shoe. That's my dog, Tige, look for him in there, too," brought the mischievous imp to life. It was part of the Saturday radio lineup of competing children's programs. Margie got all the shoe store rewards including the oxfords. Most of all she loved the "Buster Brown Show" for its eclectic collection of stories, advice, and contests.

Kid time discussions about radio program preferences were often entrenched with strong opinions that went beyond Saturday morning shows. Programs such as the *Lone Ranger*, *The Life of Riley*, and *The Great Gildersleeve* were fair fodder, as well as the mystery programs with creaking doors and scary music. That said, I was an unabashed fan of "Let's Pretend" which also broadcast Saturday morning at the same time on another station. I preferred their dramatized fairy tales with faithful reenactments of believable precision and beautiful music. "Let's Pretend" featured fairy tales, exclusively. *Cream of Wheat* was the main sponsor. Their jingle was catchy, if not compelling:

> *Cream of Wheat, it's so good to eat.*
> *And, we have it every day.*
> *Sing this song. It will make you strong.*
> *It will make you shout Hurrah!*
> *It's good for growing babies and*
> *grownups too, to eat.*
> *For all the family breakfast,*
> *you can't beat Cream of Wheat.*

I didn't particularly like Cream of Wheat, but I loved "Let's Pretend." Before there were flash-back features, if I timed it just right, I could tune into both radio programs and jiggle the dial to hear the main story on each program. That way, I was well versed for the upcoming playground debates about the best programs any particular weekend.

Selling shoes at Buster Brown was a six-day-a-week job, so Uncle Fred rows to Manette were on Sunday mornings. These trips were something of a ritual. Once landed, he would share a cup of coffee with my dad, his brother, and my mom. Often, Velma and Aubrey took part and they caught up on family news. Telephones were more the exception than the rule in those days.

It was a Sunday morning in December of 1941, a clear and brisk day that is most vivid to me. We were outside on Shore Drive somewhere between our place and my aunt and uncle's place (a good place for kids when the house is small). Aubrey was the first to notice Fred in the rowboat. The fact that he was out in such cool weather wearing a dress white shirt wasn't so unusual, but standing in the boat and waving his arms between the business of rowing wasn't the norm. "He's shouting something," Aubrey said. "What's he saying?"

Fred sat back down and rowed again. Every time he stopped to shout, he lost forward motion due to the tide. It was row and shout, row and wave... until he was close enough to Manette to be heard. "Turn on your radio! Turn on your radio! The Japs have bombed Pearl Harbor!" Fred's words were then amplified across the water. With the message delivered and acknowledged, he turned the boat around and rowed back home.

Aubrey didn't hesitate. "Turn on the radio," he echoed to my Aunt Velma. The couple who lived in the other side of the duplex came outside. Everyone was focused on the simple act of tuning into a station for the news. I certainly didn't understand the urgency or the commotion, but it frightened me.

Everything was different after that. Simply everything. My Uncle Aubrey became an Air Raid Warden and went to work in the shipyard. My dad began working double shifts at the shipyard. Rationing of some food items, gasoline and other products began. Our whole world changed that day. Our dads were absent from birthday parties, many holidays and family outings. My family listened to the radio constantly.

My cousin Margie used to say that her dad was the best looking of the Johnson brothers. I resented this statement because I thought my dad rather resembled actor George Murphy of the silver screen. In retrospect, she was probably right. Old photos of Fred depict a gentleman's gentleman—peerless features, blue eyes, and hair combed back in the style of the day. Slender, handsome, garrulous and charming, we were told. Probably an "A" personality. Fred died when Margie was just three-years old.

There must have been someplace special in Grandmother Myrtle's heart for son Fred, too. When he became ill, she rushed to Bremerton as fast as a train from Kansas could take her. He died after she arrived.

Doting and loving his little blonde daughter, Fred would always remain the perfect father. And, leaving *his Margie* so young fostered many "what if" moments for her in later years.

Yet, the image of Uncle Fred that day in December of 1941 when he frantically signaled to us the bombing of Pearl Harbor from his row boat, has never faded.

1942—visiting Stanley Park in Vancouver, BC, Canada (back l-r) Mother, Jackie, Grandmother Travilla Clark, Grandmother Myrtle Johnson, (front l-r) Monty, myself, Uncle Robert (Bobby Dean) Clark, and cousin Marjorie Johnson.

SKATING ALONG

"Ooh, what is it?'

"What's what?" my brother asked.

"Over there! Over there!"

"Over there?" he mimicked as he threw his fish line out a bit further.

"See? Ooh, it's awful. It looks mean," I whimpered, perhaps more curious than scared.

Lying on his stomach with his line in the water, Monty had a better view under the dock.

"It's a Skate. There's one under the dock most of the time," he explained.

"Even when we go in swimming?"

"Sure, but they get out of the way. They're scared of people."

I'll never forget my first sighting of a Skate as it glided near the dock on which my aunt and uncle's duplex was built. The front of their place on Shore Drive in Manette had a dock, beach and water. On the south side of their property was a big lawn with a large weeping willow tree. A white linear fence separated it from the road and the neighbor's house. Inside, their side of the duplex was compact and cute like a house boat, but one that didn't go anywhere. I probably spent more time there than at my folk's place nearby.

When we moved to Bremerton in October of 1941, my folks rented a house on the beach at 117 Shore Drive near my aunt and uncle's duplex. In those years, most of the places along the Manette's shoreline were summer cabins. Our family of five moved into one with three small rooms where I slept in my parent's bedroom. My sister and brother shared a sofa bed in the combination sunroom and dining area. The place had a bathroom with a shower but no hot water. I had the luxury of baths in a large wash tub on the kitchen floor with warm water heated on the wood stove. My bath time could include the additional excitement of any number of breezy intrusions from people tramping in and out of the only functional door in the kitchen's north wall.

Thanks to Pat, our stay in the rental was memorable, even if only a year and a bit more. Pat was my mother's terrier--loyal, smart and fun. He was a good passenger and something like entertainment on the long drive from Nebraska. Another form of entertainment was the swing my dad hung in the so-called basement of our rental. On rainy days, a collection of neighborhood kids assembled there encouraged, no doubt, by my brother. Consequently, I rarely got a turn. We had been warned to "take it easy" as it was inside and never meant to hold two or more at a time. This was promptly disregarded by the bigger boys who didn't take long to strain the joists and timbers of our cabin home and rattle the dishes in the cupboard upstairs. Once, during a particularly vigorous turn, a neighbor boy broke both speed and height records at one time. He also banged his head on the floor timber. Then, during his second attempt at a record, his head found one of the old nails used to keep the beams together. It was big, it was rusty, and it cut his scalp. It was either not completely pounded in or had worked its way out of the wood from all the vibrations. This was a sensational experience ending in stitches at the doctor's office for which my folks paid.

The boy's family seemed understanding yet mother wasn't sure how neighborly they would be after the incident. From my perspective, all seemed to go well, especially after mother said we should be more considerate of neighbors. Share our toys; invite them to get ice cream bars; the works. Since they were all older than me, her advice seemed unnecessary. Yet, I did notice the "record breaker" visited more often and seemed to gloat at his exalted status—a victim of the timber nail. He would boss and shove my brother, who was much smaller, and talked about how we better be nice to him, or else. What the "or else" was I cannot say, but I suspected later it had something to do with suing my folks for having a dangerous swing. All this coerced friendliness seemed to build day by day. Meanwhile, our dog Pat hadn't missed a beat. He often got between the "record breaker" and my brother. This meant he risked getting kicked by our guest. He barked more loudly when the boy opened the picket gate into the yard. This meant Pat had put the boy on his warning list. The two were obviously not friends.

One afternoon, a group of children were playing on Shore Drive and basking in their good fortune at having candy bars. With sugar highs all around, they dislodged wrappers and compared yumminess. In this cordial atmosphere, the "record breaker" would alternatively take a bite of his candy and then offer Pat a bite. The minute the dog got close, up the candy bar went and into the boy's mouth. This, it seems, was generally amusing. During the slow devouring of the candy, repeatedly Pat would find the bar at his level, then up again—the bar disappeared from sight. It happened once too often. Pat had legs like springs. The boy's last offer and hoist was accompanied by Pat's agile jump and a set of teeth in the boy's lip. That did it. Cries, blood, shrieks, and chaos and another trip to the doctor's office.

This time, it was Pat who paid the full price. I never knew what kind of arrangement my folks made with the neighbors, but having the dog put down was part of it. This was hard on my mother, especially since she knew the family was planning to move in a matter of weeks.

Sadly, I watched my sister and brother leave for their first day at Manette Grade School. Still, my idle hours were few. I had a new book of Rita Hayworth paper dolls with beautiful clothes that had red fuzz trim on almost every garment. This kept me busy for hours and was my introduction to real scissors with points. Add to this a certain amount of plotting to get rid of my new babysitter.

Good sitters were hard to find but that was no deterrent. My mother had only worked at Keyport a short time when I found a way to accomplish the impossible. Just before she came home from work one evening, I locked myself in her wardrobe closet, carefully keeping the lock open until I knew the door would latch. When I heard her come home and knew she was within earshot, I pounded the closet door. "Help! Help! Let me out!" with real Shirley Temple gusto. Mother opened the door and I fell

crying into her arms. Then I told a bold-face lie. "She put me in there the minute you left!"

Dumbfounded, the babysitter had a hard time defending herself against my bleary face. I am certain mother figured out the truth eventually. Either I bragged to my sister about it or she coaxed it out of me. Mother certainly knew I was unhappy with the arrangement. As it happened, she was a stay-at-home mom until I entered First Grade.

Later in life, our family would talk of those days and laugh about this incident. Yet, even today, I have mixed emotions. Mother was the consummate career woman, and her income would have moved my family up the economic ladder quicker. Did she want or did she need a reason to defer working at that time? Or, did I simply get away with it?

1942—My brother and sister, Monty and Jackie, stand with me in the front yard of our Shore Drive home on their first day of Fourth and Fifth Grade classes at Manette Grade School.

RUBBER PERFUME

My brother could wear out the soles in his shoes in a day and not because he was a busy guy. Besides his paper route, Monty biked or walked everywhere in Manette and beyond. The school playground, on its own, was fully suited to destroy any youngster's shoes in a brief time, but it was WWII. Shoes were scarce; soles were scarcer. Leather and rubber were needed in the war effort, so, more than once, my brother's shoes were reinforced with heavy cardboard. Other materials may have been used, but my dad making newspaper patterns from my brother's old shoes or boots for temporary cardboard soles was an intriguing exercise to watch.

When a supply of real rubber soles arrived at Parker Lumber and Hardware, the news spread quicker than seagulls cawing about an unattended lunch bucket. The hardware part of their business was on upper Shore Drive, a short block from our house. Here was a sprawling collection of all manner of goods displayed on tables with glass fronts and dividers. The rubber soles were at nose level. At age three or four, it was my nose.

Quickly, I associated the delight of my mother and our neighbor's discovery of the right size with the smell of rubber—and their holding up a large boot-size specimen to ask, "will this fit?" Then, on impulse, I plastered a rubber sole to my nose and took a big whiff. "Put that down! That may have been on the floor," my mother scolded. No deterrent. When she wasn't looking, I managed another quick sniff. Wonderful!

Walking home, a more detailed explanation of my bad behavior followed—something she had an abundant talent to sustain. If I had hadn't thought to cover my ears, she would probably have grabbed one of them. In almost perfect step-by-step synchronization, my mother's "lip lashing" tormented me. At that humbling moment, I didn't know that I had inherited my mother's keen sense of smell—a gift one either rewards or regrets.

I'd like to say that was the end of my rubber sniffing adventures. It wasn't. As time went by and the rationing days ended, anytime I could go with dad to the gas station, I did, especially if it was the one on Winfield directly off the Manette Bridge. They had huge stacks of new tires in their service bay where I could sneak a sniff. This rather befuddled by dad but he tended to ignore it. Then, one time I scrambled out of the car and didn't notice that my mother, sitting in the front seat, could see me with the side mirror. I sidled up to a particularly aromatic Goodyear with my nose posed. "What are you doing?" she yelled with gusto from the car window. "Get back here this instant!" With my sheepish steps to the back seat, she cranked up the volume. "What is the matter with you? You look like a dog doing that! Do you want people to think you are a dog? It's nasty!" This is where a vivid picture of a doggy face, doggy feet and doggy tail flashes into my imagination chasing a quadrant of free styling tires down the street. "Woof. Woof. This is fun!," I thought. Just, don't let mother see me smile.

Needless to say, I embarrassed her, not me with such antics. I didn't want to promise I'd never smell rubber again. Even though her scolding could level city blocks, the smell was worth it. Like most childish things, I grew out of the silly habit. This was made easier with the introduction of the new synthetic rubber. Maybe it was the same where it counted, but it just didn't have it.

The nose knows.

Right 1944—Mother, Jackie, Monty and myself in front of our house before it was moved several blocks east up East 11th Street. When my folks bought the house (but not the lot), they understood some sort of commercial building would be built on the vacated lot.
At this writing, the part of the lot not used for parking is still vacant.

LONG DOCKS, CRABS AND TIME MACHINES

My brother Monty and his friends made regular forays under the Parker Lumber dock because the tide and currents would lodge and hide the best beach treasures there in this handy but treacherous place. The dock was probably several hundred feet long. It might as well have been three miles because I never managed to get to the end when we lived right next door. First, it was always dark under the dock even on sunny days, and it smelled bad. Second, according to my brother, a dead dog or cat was sure to be there. When it came to beachcombing, my brother and his friends had perfected the art form, bragging about such factors as timing and logistics. Yes, my brother was the expert. Some years later when he "discovered" Phew Island in Dyes Inlet north of Tracyton, I was convinced our house was the temporary headquarters of a world-class explorer.

"Come on. There are neat things under the dock. But, we have to hurry because the tide is coming in," my brother said encouragingly. "There's nothing to be afraid of." So, I'd set off with great resolve but each squishy footstep after the next told me to turn back sooner than later. I couldn't keep up with them anyway and would fuss about being left behind. At three years of age, my pace was half that of the nine - and ten-year olds ahead of me. "Hey, sissy. You're a sissy," the taunts began.

The water was big. I was little, but I wasn't afraid. I respected and admired everything about the beach. It was the best playground in the world, even when mother told me to keep my shoes clean. I learned to jump from one "clean" rock to another. My brother had no such scruples. Mud, saltwater, and every kind of beach life, particularly long strands of kelp that looked like giant whips, all required his constant attention and bold approach to acquisition. He collected sand dollars, shells, rusty cans, broken bottles and a lot of repellent things that smelled up the bulkhead when left "to dry."

I could imagine the tide coming in and not being able to get back to the house. If the tide came in too far, I would be forced to walk right next to the deepest, darkest, stinkiest part of the dock. I didn't know how to get back by Shore Drive and the thought of trespass was scary, too. There were live dogs and locked gates between the road and the other beach properties. So, the Tom Boy Badge was never earned. Much later, my cousin Margie and I would make "the journey" before the dock was torn down to build an apartment complex. It was something of a triumph. And, yes, there was a dead dog.

That first winter in Manette amazed and delighted me. I loved the beach and the water. The steely gray and choppy water of Sinclair Inlet framed a complex skyline across the Port Washington Narrows. The collection of houses, stairways, buildings, ships, and the huge Puget Sound Naval Shipyard crane— appeared as miniatures from the distance. If it wasn't foggy, we could see my Uncle Fred's place almost directly across the way on Washington Beach.

Many of the Manette beach cabins were turned into year-round houses. The plumbing for those summer homes ran directly from bathrooms and kitchens to the median low tide through pipes buried just below the gravel beach surface. There were exceptions, as erosion uncovered these connections to everyday living. This sanitation system added other aromas to the low-tide experience.

The only source of heat in our Shore Drive rental was a wood cook stove in the kitchen. The remaining floor plan was a patchwork of rooms that included a living room and an anteroom big enough for a bed. What was left of a drafty sun porch, turned bedroom, after my dad renovated the bathroom. It was a rental my folks were glad to get for several reasons. Foremost among them, we were only a half block from my aunt and uncle who had bought the former coal and ferry dock that doubled as a commuter terminus between Manette to Bremerton.

My Aunt Velma took particular pride in decorating the duplex they had constructed with its shared laundry facility in back, oil heat and, later, a fireplace in the unit they used. They constructed and white-washed board fencing and planted fruit trees. A large weeping willow dominated the southeast corner. The dock was their front yard complete with a diving board and flagpole. It also had crabs in the toilet at high tide—a starling and fearful experience when kid-size. It takes resolve and steady arms to keep from falling in when your butt doesn't fit the toilet seat.

On weekends my Uncle Aubrey offered boat launch service for 25-cents a boat from their Manette Boat Rental business. He used every bit of his mechanical abilities to keep the hoist in working condition; and working on the Shore Drive property which included rebuilding the stairs leading down to their property from Upper Shore Drive.

Even though most of us children were afraid of Mr. Pfeiffer, I can't remember why. He was reclusive but so were many others in Manette. We children were loud I suppose. Shouting always worked better than talking when playing outside his windows. He yelled for us to "shut up" regularly. More than that, he was very possessive of his beach and didn't want us on it. He mellowed after my Grandma Clark moved to Shore Drive in a temporary visit from Nebraska along with my Uncle Robert (Bobby Dean) who was younger than my sister and brother. Grandma could be charming when she wanted. She quickly became his favorite unlikeable neighbor. In typical Midwestern fashion, she met the other neighbors including an ancient gentleman who lived about six houses south on Shore Drive. One day she took me to have tea with him. His house was a museum—dark and fragile. While I was seated on a stool near my grandmother, he asked me, "Do you know who President Abraham Lincoln was?"

I shook my head back and forth.

"Shame on you! He was our most famous president. When I was about your age, I sat on his lap!"

I could only imagine why this was significant. He then pointed to his prize possession, a beautiful floor clock that chimed.

"That was purchased for my mother the day I was born. That's true," he said, "just like the song." Then he asked if I knew the "My Grandfather's Clock" song. I shook my head back and forth again. I didn't know it, but he did. In a raspy voice, he sang it to us. Grandma Clark beamed. I think she thought it was grand opera.

That afternoon in a room that smelled of tea, linoleum, and life at a standstill, my combined emotions of inadequacy and admiration locked his presence in my mind. He always personified my visual memory of that old song and that old place.

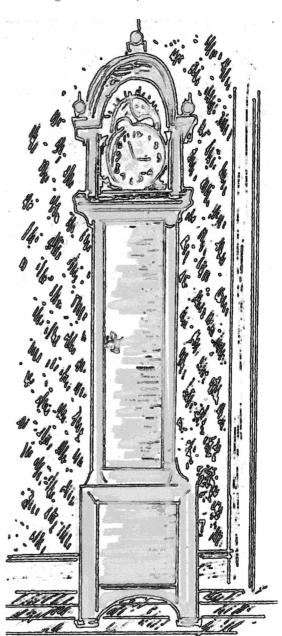

OCCUPATION BRATS

World War II gave our lives new dimensions and worries. Dads worked long hours over a period of some four years. Family fun was often brief, tired moments left over from exhausting work schedules and nerve-wracking worry. Manette looked like a military bastion. Air raid shelters were rebuilt into the retaining walls between Lower and Upper Shore Drive. An idyllic, carefree childhood playing in fields of wildflowers was reserved for the *Dick and Jane* books of our First Grade classroom.

In 1942, all the boys wanted to be Jimmy Doolittle, the flying ace who flew sorties over China, but I settled on for a turtle with a Doolittle insignia on his shell purchased from Woolworth's. Frank Sinatra kept pubescent young women like my sister fixated on their transitional youth with songs like "I want to Buy a Paper Doll" and "Always." My sister and her friends volunteered for air watch duty on the rooftops of the YMCA and the Enetai Inn in Bremerton. Yes, some children are Army Brats but we children in Manette during World War II were *Occupation Brats.*

By the time my folks moved to the house on East 11th Street, we kids were acquainted with almost all the "blimp keepers" living behind the barbed wire fence on Pitt Street. While older sisters and brothers were in school, we preschoolers watched the day-to-day military activity from our front porches. For me, it was more interesting than watching pharmacist Bill Barrington take his smoke breaks on the back porch of his store up the long flight of steps directly behind our house. No doubt, from this perch, he had full view of the extensive network of submarine nets marked by buoys in Dyes Inlet, by the Manette Bridge and well into Sinclair Inlet.

It's not easy to convey how sincerely innocent and easygoing the relationships between we neighborhood children and these older kids on the block were; more like visiting a distant relative whose memories of and homesickness for their own families prompted lots of teasing and good-natured fun. Given these facts, these GIs might still be looked upon with some suspicion today, but it was 1943 and they were a contingent of soldiers who maintained the blimp that shared a triangle piece of property nearby. This militarized zone's barbed wire fence stood in sharp contrast to grocer George Martin's white picket fence next door. It was one of many blimp bases scattered throughout the area during the war that were hasty setups but the centers of activity.

It didn't take long to become acquainted with the soldiers, but some were more noticeable than others. One was a tall, lanky kid with a quiet disposition and a carrot top crew cut. Probably only 18 or 19 at the time, he was generous with Hershey bars. His nickname was "Red" and his home state was Texas. That intrigued me more than the occasional candy bar because my Grandpa Hervie also lived in Texas. After a while, my mother relaxed her protective mode and let me meet Red's pals behind the barbwire. He carried me on his shoulders into the compound. "What is your name? I have a sister about your age," was common banter. It was here that I learned the names of other states, like Ohio and Virginia and Maine, an early introduction to US geography.

People in Manette didn't need much prompting to invite the GIs to Sunday dinner or a dockside party. Red and his pals had candy, coca-colas and cigarettes, but considered invitations to have dinner at nearby homes a treat. Most enlisted men would bring butter or some tinned meat to add to the meal—a fair trade in commodities for a chance to sit on a sofa, play Parcheesi or Canasta, and enjoy the company of civilians. My mother would comment on their good manners and thankful attitudes. Home style cooking made up in flavor what it lacked in volume or variety due to wartime rationing.

Uncle Aubrey invited crewmembers from an English frigate that had come to PSNS for repairs and kept in contact with them during their stay in Bremerton.

Familiar songs around the piano were our homemade entertainment. "Coming in on a Wing and a Prayer and "Over There" were among my favorites, but Red preferred "Yellow Rose of Texas." Fine with me. My grandpa Hervie Harrington had taught me all the words!

At night, with the blackout in force, I would sometimes hear the drone of a single engine airplane overhead. I then would pull the covers tightly over my head and say a fervent prayer that it was one of "ours."

1944 Brother Monty and I after our house was moved to the corner of East 11th and Vandalia. The Beathe family lived in the neighbor's house shown behind us. It was later the home of the Robert and Nel Block family.

Red and his pals began to leave before the official end of WWII and left many reminders of their stay behind. No blimps, but among them were the buildings that later became part of the Manette Playground and Senior Center between Nipsic and Vandalia at East 13th Street. While adults set about finding some normality in their lives after the war, we children missed Red and his pals. It seems appropriate to remember them as "friendly invaders" who occupied not only Manette, but our hearts for a time.

Story time

Children are interested in stories, particularly about the people they know. At least, I was. Grandmother Myrtle Johnson understood this. I can only guess that she used her remarkable storytelling ability to entertain and inform her own children. This offered them an oral history of her childhood, her relatives known and unknown , and the times she lived when young. When asked about her family, such as her sister Diamond Pearl (for who could resist wondering about a lady with a name like that), Myrtle was generous with the bits and parts she thought we could absorb. The amazing thing about her stories was that she always told the same stories in the same way—never embellishing them or retracting the storyline. I could listen to her for hours and probably did.

Mark Stevens , who lived with my folks for 18 years, was another great storyteller; however, he rarely talked from his own experiences, even when pressed to do so. Instead, he told wonderful, magical and adventurous stories. Again, usually in exactly the same way to such an extent that if he tried to shorten a story so he could do something else or he simply forgot a part, he would be urgently reminded to rewind and set it right. Such were the major early influences and genteel reminders of the importance of little stories. Later, a couple of my grade school teachers come to mind, especially the ones who read to our class and selected books that kept us anxious to know what happened next. Contrast this with the typical response of most grownups to a simple questions like, "what was it like when you were little?" or "where did you live when you were my age?"

"Oh, I don't know. That was a long time ago." Or, "I'm busy, go ask your father." Answers like those raised more questions, especially when told "you wouldn't understand." Or "why do you want to know about that old stuff? Haven't you got better things to do?" I was curious. If I wasn't interested, I wouldn't have asked. Inside, I am shouting, "Find a way to tell me about you in a way I can under-

stand!" No luck. My foray into reporting and newspaper publishing in the Fourth Grade would have turned out better if I had received more cooperation. It would have been nice if someone had noticed the impossible task of typing each issue of the Manette News singly. When I completed three issues, I gave up.

I liked stories because they were digestible, and helped me process and store information in ways I could recall—something like a file cabinet with all the appropriate labels—stories are the labels that help us remember the who, the what and the when. I would pretend there was a disk jockey in my brain who recorded everything I saw and heard. He would then make a record of this and play it back when I needed the information. I drew cartoons of him and the recording studio.

We were curious children with little restraint in the imagination sector. When unversed about what happened behind closed doors, we often fashioned our own, more colorful, version.

When my folks bought the house on the corner lot of East 11th Street and Shore Drive in 1944, they knew it would be moved to make way for some sort of commercial development. Across the street was Etten's Market and the new and groovy Stan's Drive-In. Directly behind the house was Barrigan's Drug Store and Doolies Ice Cream Parlor on Harkins. A small apartment complex was on the right. Someone had big plans for that property, yet, after the house was moved, it sat empty for decades and remains so. After looking at several locations including East 18th, my folks decided to move the house to a corner lot on East 11th several blocks east. My mother knew that street lights and sidewalks were planned for the length of East 11th Street, and that East 18th Street was darkly outside the city limits.

Getting ready for the house move was exciting and unnerving for me. Most of our furnishings stayed in the house. We had the job of putting our things into dresser drawers which were subsequently laid down on the floor. In my mind's eye I can still see the house lumbering past Scott Street and Aldrich's Variety Store slowly inching its way to its new destination. I was so anxious that my dolls might not survive the trip. We had to wait for some days until the house was stabilized on concrete blocks and a new foundation poured and set before we could check on our stuff. There was some minor window breakage but the most important stuff, my toys and dolls, were okay. Whew!

It was from this location that I entered Kindergarten taught by Mrs. Buckley. It was located in the basement of the Manette Community Church and associated with the Bremerton School District. Either district funding was limited or not available because our families paid tuition, something in the range of $15 a quarter for a half day Monday through Friday. I loved everything about Kindergarten except naptime. I didn't take naps at home; why did I have to have them at school? Besides, I was too excited to nap. I'm sure this nap-rest time gave our teacher a bit of a respite, but I was eager to finger paint or learn a new game. On cold days, I came home to "Welsh Rabbit" until mother went to work.

It's probably not fair to include my Kindergarten class photo when all the students names can't be properly listed. It was taken by a parent after our Christmas party in 1944, and captures our expressions on a wintery day before Christmas break. We are on the steps of Manette Community Church (our Kindergarten classroom was in the basement) as mostly happy children with some younger siblings peaking out from behind our bundled-up bodies. Besides our exchange gift, we received a stocking with rationed candy.

Faces I recognize include Betty Forehand, Ruth Peterson, Clayton Gorst, Carol Jacobs, Scott Harrington, Mickey Selementi, Betty Roberts, George LeCompte, Sherri Frazer, Dale Hammergren, Elizabeth Roberts, Marilyn Jacobsen, Sandra Fisher and Barbara Bowers. I am in the back row (second from right) with the Pompadour bangs and white scarf.

Note: Mrs. Buckley, our teacher, is without a head in this photograph.

THE MANETTE BRIDGE—

BEARER OF MEMORIES AND MISFORTUNE

With an aunt and uncle living on Washington Beach (Bremerton) and another aunt and uncle plus my family on the Manette (East Bremerton) side, walking across the Manette Bridge was a regular occurrence. Once, on our way home, my mother and I were near the Bridge when I told her I wanted a hundred children. It seemed like a good number. "I think you'll find that many are more than you can take care of," she replied, avoiding the more obvious, adult reason. Through a series of exchanges, she whittled my expectations to ten. I thought about this as we passed the wood plank railings on the bridge and I ran my hand along their interesting texture. "Stop doing that. You'll ruin your gloves and get splinters," she warned. I pulled my hand back and noticed the dirty smudges on my white glove fingertips.

We could count on the Manette Bridge for encounters of all kinds, scary moments and as a retreat of sorts—for its understructure wasn't a place where adults cared to tread. When my Grandmother Travilla was living in Manette with my Uncle Bob (Bobby Dean), they stayed about a year. During this time, she had her gallbladder removed. While my mother and Aunt Velma helped Grandmother with her recovery, my brother was charged with Bobbie's "recreation and welfare," otherwise known as keeping him busy.

To my brother's eleven-year-old rationale, this meant Bobbie could tag along with him and his pals. For their adventurous spirits, it was an easy climb onto the wooden support timbers of the original Manette Bridge. Here a contingent of pre-teens and older guys would use the timbers to walk out as far as the first concrete pylons, drop their fishing lines and smoke. From any vantage point along the shore, the guys could be identified using binoculars and called home. On one such occasion, and perhaps

the first for Bobby Dean, they came back to Aunt Velma's place to find Grandma propped in the living room. She immediately asked Bobby Dean to come over and give her a kiss. That was girly stuff and he was reluctant. Seems she wanted to smell his breath as she was more concerned about him smoking than falling off the Bridge.

There was a fatality fall from the Manette Bridge a couple years later. Monday through Saturday, Manette-side newspaper boys walked to Bremerton to pick up their newspaper bundles, then walked back to distribute papers on their afternoon routes. Our newspaper carrier was one of them; a nice kid who lived with his parents and brother down the block and around the corner on Trenton Avenue. He probably wasn't the first kid to walk the flat-top fence railing on the original bridge, but a hearsay report indicated there was a challenge to do just that. With a width of six- to eight-inches, the rail-walk may have seemed an easy dare to meet. Instead, he fell and died. It was a terrible tragedy for all concerned and a hard, tearful lesson. The family moved away a short time later. I'd like to think the plans to update and upgrade safety on the Bridge in 1949 may have been influenced by this death, but more likely it was the twenty years of use that prompted it.

While the Manette Bridge was undergoing improvements in the early 1950s, our entertainment and social life deteriorated. The Saturday movie matinee was a tradition of long standing. As soon as our Saturday chores were finished, we were off to the Admiral, the Roxy, or the Tower Theaters— whichever one was running the best deal, a double feature complete with cartoons and sometimes serial feature. My quarter allowance covered admission (15-cents) and money for pop corn (10-cents). Occasionally, some financial strategies were employed like sharing pop corn for half a Mounds Bar.

I don't recall if they closed the Bridge to vehicle traffic at that time. Maybe not, it would have been a twenty-mile drive via Silverdale to reach Bremerton. For my generation, the big inconvenience was when the Bridge was closed to foot traffic. We couldn't go to the movies! After two or three weeks of that non-sense, foot traffic resumed, but with a caveat. The Manette Bridge walk became a treacherous, heroic journey. At various locations, but not all, pedestrians had to walk on a sturdy foot-wide plank, secured at both ends.

When we learned the Bridge was open again, it took some convincing to assure my mother that it was perfectly safe to go to the movies. She offered some assurance of her own with these famous words: "Hold on to each other's hands." No way. We needed both of them, one for each side-by-side railing.

We used the wobbly handrails nailed on both sides of the plank. From this perch, we could see the water swirling below waiting for us to take one false step. This arrangement was moved from place to place as work progressed. For me, a rainy day and some wind increased the fear factor. Nevertheless, my interest in seeing the latest movie was greater than my trepidation.

Those crossings generated a host of scary dreams in years to follow, each with some variation on the theme of rickety boards across the Port Washington Narrows and falling into its water far, far below. These dreams would scare me awake. Once my pounding heart had calmed a bit, I'd go downstairs as quick as I could and get in bed with my parents. How sardonic to blame such an iconic structure for these childish fears.

Could it be that instinct told me the original Manette Bridge was basically an attractive nui-sance? That it was used and abused by the younger citizens in a time when safety and danger were on equal footing? Surely hundreds of children have had experiences such as this, either with the Manette Bridge or one like it. That said, I wouldn't have traded them at the time for a safer passage, nor would I today.

1944—Uncle Robert (Bobby Dean) Clark, sister Jackie (probably trying to keep me in place), and brother Monty at the Monson duplex on Shore Drive.

BIRDS, BEES & BACKYARD MOLES

While she lived only two houses and one street away, Janet's home was quite different from mine. She lived quietly with her mother, sister, and grandmother. I lived noisily with my sister and brother, parents, our boarder and all manner of visiting relatives and friends whose extended stays meant I never knew when I had to give up my bedroom and sleep on the couch.

Like the moles in her mother's garden, I was the persistent pest who showed up at the door to ask, "Can Janet play?" Basically, Janet and I got along fine and her mother tolerated me but occasionally, I would come home upset about some part of our "unbalanced" friendship. After her father had died, Janet sought my company briefly and with such dignity. Once, during this time, her mother actually called me to come over to "distract" her. It seems the ambulance that had taken her father away also took part of her childhood.

I was also the young, nearby and appreciative recipient of Janet's hand-me-downs. One such outfit, a stunning red and blue shirt and matching vest, almost ended our friendship. While waiting for our home-service dry-cleaner, the outfit lay on a bookcase at my house where the cat decided it would make a nice bed. Janet saw this and told her mother. Her mother scolded me saying I didn't appreciate nice things. I told my mother. My mother thought Janet's mother was snooty and unreasonable. I think she called Janet's mother to tell her this. With our friendship once again intact, the outfit became my favorite. After I grew a couple inches in height, it became my beautiful ice-skating costume.

Janet had red hair, freckles and, at age nine, an air of frugal superiority she truly deserved. I thought everything about Janet was wonderful, but especially her dolls. It was my best one-sided friendship because she was older and so wise. And, there were the dolls in her attic: a treasure trove of beautiful dolls given to her and her older sister, most of which were still in their original boxes—a mystery I could never understand.

There was one important exception to her world of exiled dolls. Janet loved to play with her miniature dolls and the quaint hand carved and overstuffed furniture, some of which had been in her family for years. The dolls were porcelain look-alike little beauties with cropped hairstyles right out of a vintage magazine. With bodies of childish proportions, their only claims to animation were moveable arms. To our credit, we were both accomplished at playing *a cappella*, namely, without a dollhouse.

I drew elaborate house plans on butcher paper and taped them to a drawing board. The linoleum pattern in the "kitchen" alone might take me an hour to execute in colored pencil or crayon. Janet preferred a box or simply using little squares of fabric rugs to define the rooms. We spent a lot time describing what was to be imagined in each of the varied setups: gardens, walls with paintings, and other necessities. We often played on her backyard sidewalk next to the lawn swing with earwigs. Janet's mother had a clear view of us there, but perhaps more importantly, she had a clear view of her garden. She was always on mole patrol. More than once, she would come running out of the house with a shovel only to curse a failed attempt to nab one of the tunnel-making nuisances.

"Please, come play at my house," I repeated almost every time we spread our Lilliputian domiciles across the floor of her bedroom or in her backyard during warm weather. Only once, in the several years we faithfully play-acted the roles of her all-female household and my moveable, plastic, gender-balanced people, did Janet agree to travel the two houses and one street away to play on my front porch.

"Helen and Harry, and Betty and Bob are thrilled you could visit," I spoke in my mother doll voice convincingly, tap-tapping her along. "Thank you, but we cannot stay long," Janet's mother doll replied. "I have company coming, so this visit will have to be brief." And, it was. Consequently, we spent most of our play time at her house. That meant I had to tote several boxes back and forth, but that was okay.

On the surface, life was serene at Janet's house with a sense of history. Her grandmother who read and did crossword puzzles using a magnifying glass intrigued me. Her sister was beautiful, popular and sported a tan. They had a real dining room and a heated basement with a clothes drying rack. Compare this to the ongoing barrage of relatives and assorted friends who traipsed through, ate meals, and otherwise "hung out" at my house with sheets hung across the laundry room and kitchen to dry during wet weather. Janet would not have been comfortable at one of our noisy Friday night chili feeds. Add to this the fact that my aunt Kay, cousins, and grandmother lived right next door to her. Janet was curious about them, and us, but still preferred second-hand reports, which I gladly provided.

One late summer morning, we were picking plums from their backyard tree using them for "food" as we played "house" in the three-sided outside room next to the garden. Her mother was in a particularly good mood having dispatched an offending mole that very day, an act of horrible admiration. "It must have been rabid... poking its head up this time of day," she explained as she went inside the kitchen door. Maybe, she was right.

Out of the blue, figuratively and literally, Janet said, "Do you know where babies come from?" "Of course, I know," I replied. "My mother told me they grow inside. She even showed me her tummy once where I grew before I was born."

"Well, that's not what I mean," Janet continued.

Now, we rarely, if ever, spoke in hushed tones, but Janet did lower her voice when she continued, "I know how babies get there in the first place.

1945 Janet and I wear corsages for Easter church service.

They don't just start growing on their own, but maybe I shouldn't tell you."

"Why?"

"Because you are too young."

"Oh, please tell me. Please. Please. I am not too young. Why should this be a secret, anyway?"

" 'Cause I might get in trouble if I tell."

"I won't tell anyone else, honest."

"Promise?"

"Promise."

"A man puts his thing in a woman. That's how babies get started."

"Ugh. You're kidding me."

"No, it's true."

"That's icky." As I thought about it, I just about fell over from this surprise revelation.

"See, I told you, you are too young."

My daddy came to mind and every man I knew who I respected and loved. I couldn't imagine them doing this. My mother, too? Where, how? I wanted to cry.

"Everybody," Janet calmly said, "Everybody started the same way."

There was no deterring her. If this was the truth and if I didn't believe her, then I was a dimwit. Later, as I walked home I felt like Janet's secret was ever so-o-o heavy. It hung across my shoulders like a boulder.

As I trudged along the warm sidewalk, I saw my dad cutting the grass. A flood of emotions (anger, curiosity, and disbelief) made my face flush. It must have showed.

"Are you okay?" he said. "What's wrong?"

"Nothing." Only the thought of the whole world making babies the same way made my naiveté crumble away with each step.

For some time later, people on the streets, pictures of people in *Life Magazine*, voices on the radio, were all reminders of this singular truth.

As we grew older, we saw less of each other. The year before Janet went off to a school for girls in Tacoma, sometimes we played in the two-room basement apartment at her house, when it wasn't rented. Janet was particularly curious about one young couple who moved in after their marriage. More than once, she would unlock the apartment door to see their belongings. We would talk about whether they ever— "did it"—because Janet thought he was dreamy. She had to be careful because the bathroom was across the hall and the apartment had two separate entrances. I was the lookout.

Sometimes I wonder what ever happened to Janet and think where else would you find a young friend willing to help build a Golden Carriage? After several hours working only with dreams and without plans, we managed to clumsily nail two weather-beaten boards together before we gave up. Who else could have given me such an apt introduction to Ella Fitzgerald vocals on 45 rpm records, or teach me the importance of timing when watching for the arrival of the Bremerton High School boys basketball team at Coach Wills' house on the corner? Besides, any young friend who shares the perfect Mud Pie recipe must be trusted with life's secrets. Of course, I later told my friends Barbara and Shelly how babies start. I got in trouble, but it was worth it.

PLAYTIME REVISITED—

A SCENARIO

"It's time for Harry to come home from work. He will be so surprised to see how the front room has been rearranged," said Helen in her loving homemaker voice.

Janet adjusted the small red vase of flowers on the miniature baby grand piano.

I picked up Harry where he had been laid on the grass earlier, while "at work." His dark blue plastic suit, unrumpled and perfect as ever, and his neat red tie made him look every bit the businessman

despite the slight wearing of skin colored paint from his face and hands, the result of daily adventures with his dollhouse family and friends. His moveable legs bounced slightly as he walked in through the invisible, but oh-so-real front door.

"My goodness, Helen, you've been busy today," he exclaimed to his dollhouse wife.

Playing dollhouse was an obsession with Janet, my older (by two and a half years) neighbor girl and me in the years between 1945 and 1950. Janet's dollhouse was small but elegant. It had a front room, dining room, and kitchen on the main floor. There were two bedrooms on the second. The windows were covered with a sturdy waxed paper that boasted real-looking windowpanes. The walls in each room had tiny floral designs and decorations such as paintings, wall lights, and mirrors befitting the motif. Her furniture was wooden in simple design, delicate looking but well into the second generation of use. The house had been a gift to her older sister many years earlier. A rare item today, no doubt a delight in 1947.

My "dollhouse" was very different because it was simply a floor plan I drew on butcher paper that was supplied by Roy and Glen's Market in Manette. I drew it in pencil and carefully colored it with crayons, complete with linoleum squares in the kitchen and bath and a newspaper on the door stoop. I preferred this "dollhouse" to the metal one I got for Christmas shortly after World War II. The metal house was pre-printed in ghastly colors; it was held together by little tabs that either wouldn't or couldn't stay put or broke off entirely. But the worst thing was all the busy, ugly printed things on the walls that didn't match my furniture or my fine-tuned sense of aesthetics at age six.

The best features of my dollhouse collection were my furniture pieces and accessories. They were the latest plastic toys from *Ideal* and included a blue vacuum, a red and cream telephone with a twist cord, a dishwasher that really opened and held tiny plastic dishes, and a high chair that converted into a play rocker for my small rubber baby.

It didn't matter that the couch and chairs were plastic. My plastic people never complained because they always got a good night's rest. I had made them beds from tissue boxes and used pieces cut from my brother's socks for their cozy blankets. Likewise, my mother's trunk of fabrics was not spared in my search for suitable bedcovers.

For two young girls, our dollhouse people had the best of both worlds. Janet's dollhouse had charm and stability, while I drew a new "house" almost every week and outfitted it with the latest items mother bought for me at Woolworth. The collection was my treasure.

Our favorite days were in the warm, dry summertime when we could set up our things in the shade of fruit trees in Janet's backyard. A backyard her mother worked in regularly. Janet liked to stay in her own yard, and it was an agreeable place. Her mother tended their garden and flowerbeds while we set up our time consuming and complicated miniature stages of drama. While neighbors on three sides were busy with their properties, while carpenters built a garden house one summer in the corner of Janet's backyard, and other people who rented the basement apartment at her house came and went, the lives of my miniature people—Harry and Helen and their children Bob and Betty plus their once-in-a-while rubber baby—went on undisturbed.

Janet's people were little China dolls only three inches high and not quite true to the one-inch equals one-foot scale. She loved them. Her favorite was a wavy-haired brunette who wore a band around her head reminiscent of the Thirties, her probable vintage. Only their arms moved so their gowns were simple chemise outfits that slipped over their tiny bodies. They could be tied or untied with a length of narrow ribbon. Janet's dolls changed names as often as they changed dresses. Her clothes included a fur-trimmed coat that was kept in a small cedar chest. Janet made quite a production out of these costume changes!

My family members never changed clothes. Their uninspired outfits were part of their plastic personalities. The best I could manage was a red printed crinkle crepe nightgown I made for Helen, hand stitched and unbecoming. Just a minor frustration in the world of dollhouse play with big ideas and child-size skills.

What did small China dolls and bendable plastic dolls do during these years? The themes were domestic and ordinary, often remakes from radio shows, books or movies. Rarely were they re-enactments from the lives of any real people or families.

"Yes," Helen said. "Doesn't it look lovely? Our good neighbor Margaret here (Janet's doll) gave me the idea to put the couch just so and your favorite chair (the red fabric overstuffed wing chair) by the fireplace. I hoped you would be pleased."

Harry and Helen sat down in the living room with their practical bendable knees, feet firmly planted on the crayoned carpet. Margaret stood nearby on her straight China legs, smiling.

SOMETHING IN MY POCKET

There's something in my pocket.
It belongs across my face.
I keep it very close to me in a most convenient place.
In case you may be wondering,
you could guess a long, long while.
So, I'll take it out and put it on…
it's a great big Brownie smile.

Almost all the girls in my class belonged to our Manette Brownie Troop, so a large contingent of giddy girls skipped to Mrs. Buell's on Monday afternoons after school. Those were special days at Carla Rae's house during the school year. We tried to be nice to each other while we sang, played games, and learned how to make things. Making important things, too, like woven cording. We took turns with a hammer and pounded tiny nails into the edges of empty thread spools. We were shown how to pass string or yarn around the nails and push the knotted mess through the hole with a pencil. As the cord became longer, it could be easily pulled from below the spool with two fingers. Closing off the cording to prevent unraveling was the hard part.

When Mrs. Buell told us she would not be our leader the next year, my world dropped out of sight. It was like school without a playground or my doll without any clothes. Others took over and we pressed on to earn our various badges and maintain our Brownie smiles, even if they were hidden a little deeper in our pockets.

Mrs. Selementi, Mickey's mom, led our troop for most of a year. Besides being gregariously kind and offering some of the best treats we'd ever had, Mrs. Selementi made it clear she was only subbing until a permanent leader could be found. One fascinating item at their house was their player piano—or a hybrid of some kind. Mrs. Selementi explained and showed us how the magical contraption altered the piano's soundboard, then allowed each of us to touch a single key. It was a thrilling.

When we heard that Mrs. Gray would become our new leader, there was a communal shrug. We wondered whose mother she might be. Later, we thought it was unusual that she had no daughters.

Her son Chad was older and we rarely saw him. Our apprehension dissolved quickly at the first meeting because Mrs. Gray thought of us as her Brownie daughters. She led our Troop with discipline and affection. Like a promo for a movie, she would often tease us with a preview of our project for the next week. We could hardly contain our excitement. It was in this setting that we made "camp stoves" using a large coffee can and GI surplus Sterno. We fried an egg on it in the backyard. It was so effective we immediately tested them out on the tent caterpillars we found there. She was shocked at this experiment but never scolded us for our ingenuity.

After an initial flush of enthusiasm, the main reason I stayed in Girl Scouts was to go to summer camp. This meant I had to maintain reasonable attendance and complete a certain number of badges in any given year. After she moved to Manette, my cousin Margie joined our troop and faithfully attended the meetings. Yet, as the school year progressed, she convinced me that we might have better things to do with the five-cent dues our parents gave us each week. To avoid a trek of multiple blocks, we would sneak past the meeting place, the community building on the Manette Playground. We would slowly crouch lower than the log bulkhead between the sidewalk on East 13th Street, which was above the open field and past the tennis courts. We did this so we could go to my house first and raid the refrigerator. This gave us enough energy to take our ill-gotten gains to the variety store or ice cream shop. After a few weeks of this and a buildup of red ink in our troop ledger, we ran out of excuses to tell our scout friends and our leader. Margie raided her piggy bank to make up the deficit. I begged a quarter from my dad and made up some excuse about losing the money—each week! Obviously, we both had much to learn about living the Girl Scout oath. Obviously, we couldn't be trusted to sell Girl Scout cookies door-to-door.

The previous summer, I had gone to scout camp and gave the week-long experience at Lake Bennetson two thumbs up despite the long and bumpy ride on dirt and gravel roads, and my dad's concern about breaking an axle. Aunt Dorothy, Margie's mom, took us to Dr. Biedel for the required physical checkup. What I didn't realize was that Margie had trepidations about "roughing it" as she had never lived in the wilderness or gone camping before. But, she packed her sleeping bag and gear and put on a brave face.

We joined other girls from Kitsap and Mason County for a glorious week of archery, swimming, and boating. We did various crafts, learned about the solar system without the distraction of streetlights, and ate lots of pancakes. Camp also meant outdoor toilets and sleep deprived nights because there were mosquitoes without number, scary stories, and Loons that sounded like wolves in the distance.

Tough as she tried to appear, Margie was petrified of the wilderness and wouldn't go to the outhouse after dark, even though she had the biggest flashlight in our tent. She whined about everything. She cried herself to sleep at night more often than not. I should have been more sympathetic because I wasn't very brave myself. Instead, I was annoyed and perplexed that she wasn't having a good time. This was the first and last time she came with me.

I enjoyed Girl Scout camp again the following summer and became quite proficient at archery. My brother rewarded my enthusiasm and gave me his bow and arrow set. Despite the bales of straw used as a backdrop, the neighbors complained about the stray practice arrows that landed in their yards from time to time. Mother put a stop to this Robin Hood personae rather quickly.

Our Brownie troop gathered at the Buell home included (back row) three unknown girls, then Judith Hawes, Shelly, me, Barbara Bowers, Sandra Fedt, and Sherri Frazer. (front row) Laurie Sue Espen, Carla Rae Buell, Marilyn Jacobsen, Mickey Selementi, Aladean Calhoun, Sandra Fisher, Carol Jacobs, Elsie White, and Myra Ellen Calhoun.

THE AQUA HOUSE CONSPIRACY

We shoved and giggled as we knelt on the cool linoleum floor, each of us trying to peek into the keyhole with nine-year-old eyes. Both of our noses were next to the worn key-hole in the locked door, trying in tandem to see the other side. One shove and Margie had it in her sights, tilting her head side to side as she squinted. Surely her thick glasses were an advantage in situations like this.

"I can't see a thing," she whispered, exasperated.

"Shh," I motioned, finger to lips.

"Who's there?" Mark called out. "I can hear you!"

He said he was going to take his afternoon nap. We had planned this maneuver all summer; we were determined to find the "truth." We wanted to see if Mark could walk. Suddenly Pepper, our black Labrador, came bounding through the open door, toes a-tap-tapping on the floor.

"Who's there?" Mark said again.

"It's just Pepper," I confessed.

"What are you girls doing?"

"Just playing with Pepper."

"Let's run. He knows we're here," said Margie speaking very softly.

"No... let's wait," then we heard the unmistakable sounds of Mark getting into his wheelchair. Time to make our escape! To avoid being seen, we ran outside and hid by the corner of the large front porch, then jumped, slid, and flopped onto the bank of grass above the sidewalk with Pepper, our trusty accomplice, in tow. We were out of breath by the time we got there.

"That was close! Did you see anything?"

"Nothing, didn't see a thing," Margie replied.

We stretched out on the grass that July afternoon, cousins only six months apart in age with six weeks until school started. With youthful delusion, we thought our antics held special significance, like snooping at Mark's door. Glad for the rest, Pepper groomed himself in his typical, favorite man-dog fashion, while we talked quietly and picked blossoms off the neighbors snowball bush, tossing bits

and pieces, looking our nonchalant best. Secret discussions fueled a cauldron of suspicion. With each re-telling the entire diabolical scheme unfolded again, whetted by evidence both pure and circumstantial.

Past the parking strip with two spindly Elm trees, where dad parked our '39 Chevy sedan, and across the street lived the neighborhood "commander," the person who directed all the Aqua-House cohorts. As ordinary things happened nearby—a lawn being cut by a rotary mower, the distinct vibrations from the ferry headed for Seattle, and the sounds of a hammer forging neighbor Beath's new basement room—we waited for extraordinary things to occur. Spies had to be patient. That was good detective work.

In that summer of 1948, Margie and I experienced a "revelation," so we sleuthed to prove our complicated theory about people who lived in aqua houses. We gathered facts prowling the streets and alleyways of Manette taking note of any aqua houses and those with aqua trim—obvious sympathizers. We debated the significance of the degree of green or blue that created the aqua blend; also an important distinction.

Margie was fair with straight blond hair that her mom forced into curls at regular intervals. Shorter and younger, she was street-wise and funny and the perfect partner for counter espionage. Since I had dark, wispy curly hair and brown eyes, we didn't look like cousins, a fact we shared and buried as suited the occasion. We both loved adventures but argued about what to do when, and to whom. If things didn't go her way, she got mad and went home. When it didn't go my way, I sulked and pouted. But that summer, we were invisible super spies stretched out on the grass watching. We were bold, self-appointed secret agents wisely wrapped in the perfect disguise, the camouflage of youth. We took mental notes. We waited. Time was on our side!

The Aqua House Command Center had an old two-ton truck parked in front that I had never seen operated. It was probably older than the roof on the neighbor's house. Maybe, he couldn't drive it anymore? Possible, because he his legs didn't work right. He still managed to hobble to the East Side Tavern every day. We knew the tavern was dark and mysterious during the day; therefore, the neighbor must have clandestine reasons to be in the dark on a summer day. Ergo—he was the leader! Made perfect sense.

Margie and I congratulated ourselves on our clever deductions and observations. We reminded each other we were the only ones to fully understand the difficult part: *how they communicated.* The secret was the color aqua. It was THEIR color, so the owners of every house in Manette painted aqua must belong to the Aqua House Conspiracy. We also knew that Mark was involved somehow and, the best part, he and the neighbor could really walk. This was a concept so profound we scared ourselves just talking about it!

As shadows fell across the street from our spying place, Margie and I diligently watched nothing happen at the neighbor's house that day—or any day for that matter. Besides, would the FBI believe a couple of kids? Impatient with inactivity, we argued over who was the best cowboy: Roy Rogers or Gene Autry. Once again, Margie made her daily offer to trade her red metal roadster (the one I had earned in a *Seattle PI* promotion and traded to her earlier) for my very special red floral, overstuffed dollhouse wing chair. "No," was my firm answer every time she asked. Whatever happened to the red roadster—so neat to spin in circles at the Manette Playground tennis courts, I never knew.

The paper boy had long since tossed the evening paper onto our front porch with Pepper in short pursuit. We heard the Navy Yard whistle sometime before Mother was let off by her car-pool driver. Soon the bus would stop in front of the boxwood hedge of the "Branch Estate," and dad would walk the half block to our front steps. Margie got up and practiced her pitching arm with an imaginary base ball.

"I'm hungry. What've you got to eat?" she asked.

"Maybe we could get some peanut butter," I answered as we walked into the kitchen where we found Mark wheeling back to his room. He momentarily blocked our way to the cupboard. Very seriously, he asked, again,

"What were you two up to today?"

"Nothing."

"Nothing."

"Were you trying to look through the keyhole on my door?"

Silence.

"Because if you were, it won't do you any good."

"Why? Oops!"

"Because," he said, carefully guiding himself over the threshold, nicking a little paint off the doorsill in the process, "I sealed off the old keyhole a long time ago." He wheeled into his room and shut the door.

In the Manette of my childhood, all colors held special meanings and messages and all cripples could walk. We just never saw it happen. That fall our mothers bought us matching rain coats we thought very suitable for our new way of life. They were French trench coats with wide lapels. They were stylish. They were aqua.

1948—East 11th Street looking East. The Nipsic Avenue intersection is on the right. Thankfully, there weren't many aqua houses.

GRASS CAKE

A 1948 COOKING CHANNEL AND
ANIMAL PLANET MERGER?

Maybe it was the Dagwood sandwiches. Perhaps the taffy-pulls. Whatever the reason, and there were many, my sister Jackie had an imaginative way in the kitchen. I know this firsthand because one summer day when she was fifteen, inspiration literally bounced across the linoleum kitchen floor and landed in a cake pan.

Like the famous multi-layered sandwich from the Blondie comic strip with husband Dagwood's foot-high version, usually with a fish peering out, my sister had tried it. Despite toothpicks and carefully selected ingredients, all the eating skills in the neighborhood couldn't keep it intact long enough to take a bite. Jackie sought to improve on these heroic towers by repeating bread slices at strategic intervals, but it didn't work much better. Undeterred and with considerable experience, she washed the kitchen floor— again.

A spiffy floor that shined like glass was an absolute must in Jackie's teenage years. It was a thankless on-your-knees task but essential for a taffy-pull party. Because the kitchen table would be pushed back against the wall, 78-rpm vinyl records would be loaded into the Philco radio-record player console and dancing would round out the evening. These parties were for teenagers only. I could only peek from the stairs or tiptoe down to the only bathroom, very often, to catch a glimpse of the latest dance steps. It was all very grown-up. If I was sufficiently sneaky, I wouldn't hear her complain, "Mom... there she is again watching us!"

One lazy day in August, Jackie asked if I wanted to make a cake. "Of course!" I asked, what flavor? "Lemon, chocolate... something out of a box?"

"I have a better idea. Let's make an *Anything Cake*." This was unexpected.

"Yes," she continued thoughtfully. "A cake is for exceptional bakers. The key to its success is the 'anything' part."

With confidence, she noted that she had enough kitchen experience to try it, but she also cautioned that this was not amateur stuff and kids, like me, should never try to make one alone.

"It will be fun," she reassured, "and maybe delicious."

"Maybe?"

"It all depends on how good an apprentice you are," she added, pulling bowls from the cupboard. I was to be her apprentice! My help was important. I was sold.

Stacking cake pans and a box of wax paper on the counter, Jackie continued with her instruction.

"The essential ingredient is originality. The baker should feel unrestrained in the selection of ingredients. The baker should feel unrestrained in the order in which they are mixed. The baker should feel unrestrained period. The idea is to be creative, daring, to be a culinary libertine."

Lots of big words, I'm thinking. Whatever it's called, a project with my sister was a fun idea all by itself.

Then she added, "did I mention it's also a good time to clean out the refrigerator?"

The word got around. Monty, our brother, was curious but remained aloof. Mark, our "relative border" and wheelchair bound was the only adult in the house at the time. He was informed that genius was about to visit the kitchen. After some basic warnings, he remained in the background-- soon to be one of our resident tasters. Mixing bowl at the ready, we first added the usual things: flour, sugar, baking powder, chocolate. Then, the exotics: molasses, steak sauce, canned peach juice, orange juice, and chopped up licorice candy. The oven was set to pre-heat and the pans prepared with lard and a dusting of flour. We took turns stirring the murky brown-colored mixture and smelling the bowl.

Then, we did the finger taste test. "Hum...needs something else," Jackie said thoughtfully. I agreed. "Wonder what?" Just about then, I glanced outside the backdoor to see our dog Pepper tearing and eating grass that was growing along side the patio.

"Look at Pepper! How about grass? He likes it a lot. We never eat grass but if animals can eat grass, then it should be in this cake."

"Okay by me," Jackie answered. Only, very important, we have to wash it first," she said, now the sanitary expert as well. Therefore, I picked grass blades of various lengths, avoiding the exact spot where Pepper ate, and carefully washed each one. My sister chopped these into small bits and added them to the mixture. "When this is baked, you won't even know grass is in it, but don't tell," she said. "It will be our secret ingredient."

"Can we call it *Grass Cake,* then?" I asked.

"I guess so, but to everyone else it's an 'Anything Cake'." How thrilling—not only to bake an original cake—but to think up a suitable, secret name, too.

"Can't forget the eggs," my sister said with authority. We looked through the refrigerator and again pondered other possibilities: jam, milk, leftover gravy. "Let's use them all," I suggested, moving along into the right mood. Once added, Jackie took over the stirring as the batter volume increased. She swiped through the lumps and liquid with a big wooden spoon while other less memorable ingredients probably found their way into the mix as well.

Jackie poured the batter into the pan. The baking time, although indeterminate, seemed to take forever. The kitchen, already warm, became substantially warmer as the afternoon sun came through the window. Finally, with the clean toothpick test telling us it was baked through, Jackie removed the *Grass Cake* from the oven to cool. We discussed the frosting, but showing good sense, she suggested we taste it before the frosting flavor and color selection. By then, we were getting a little tired of baking anyway, so we set about to clean away the evidence and dutifully wash and dry assorted containers and utensils before mother came home from work.

Once cool, the cake fell on to the plate easily. Slid and bounced out might best describe it. That was our first hint of its unusual character. It was VERY springy. A finger pressed into it made an impression as foam rubber. Jackie sliced a bit off the side for each of us. We stood looking at each other.

"Down the hatch!"

Yuk! It was awful. I dropped part of my piece as I gagged on the revolting flavor and the strong aftertaste. It literally bounced when it hit the floor. "Look at that!"

"Looks like fun," Jackie said. She cut off a bigger piece and raised her arm, giving the morsel greater height than me before dropping it. The *Grass Cake* bounced even more. Monty mimicked her. It may not taste good, we agreed, but it had plenty of play appeal with this bounce feature.

All the while Pepper watched from the back porch perplexed but completely attentive to the excitement and the mess we were making in the kitchen. In a quick leap, he was there and snatched one of the springy balls of cake, then turned to run outside with my brother right behind him. "He loves it," Monty shouted back to us as Pepper gulped down the *Grass Cake*; then looked expectedly for more.

"Guess we know who gets the rest," Jackie said.

I can't recall how much cake we fed Pepper that day, but I am pleased to report he survived it. At times, I think Pepper expected us to feed him another *Grass Cake* one day. He couldn't know that was impossible. Our *Grass Cake* that summer of 1948 was more than a doggy treat. It was a one-of-a-kind baking adventure and a daring experiment. It was culinary anarchy.

Pepper was a good sport when it came to food. Here we are on the front porch with Pepper in one of his more relaxed poses.

Mark My Words

Kids are on the periphery of family life when it comes to the why of things. My mindset at age six may not have understood the details but anything that impacted my life caught my attention. The day Mark came to our house is one I remember well. Partly, because my mother had prefaced his visit with several advance notices. Such as, "this gentleman uses a wheel chair."

"Why," I asked.

"Because his legs don't work."

"Why don't they work?"

"Because he had Infantile Paralysis as a young man."

"What is that?"

Did I mention details? A couple of weeks before Mark arrived, preparations were underway. He would use the front bedroom. He would need his meals on a tray. We must respect his privacy and, most importantly, we needed to be quiet and avoid playing outside his bedroom window because he slept during the day. Yikes! I was half-afraid of him already but my mother assured me he was a nice person.

I thought of Mark's visit as something of an adventure, since my family had hosted every family member for miles around at one time or another—uncles, cousins, all manner of relatives and friends of relatives, too. Extra people in our house and at our dinner table were not unusual.

When my mother worked in the Navy Yard supply department, she met a co-worker. The woman had an invalid relative, perhaps a brother-in-law, who lived with her family. As I understood it, the woman wanted to move to California but needed someone to take care of Mark until she got settled there.

Despite her snappy attitude at times, my mother was a softy when it came to the unfortunate. Apparently, they made arrangements for Mark to stay with us for what was only supposed to be a month or six-weeks. After her co-worker went south, she never contacted my mother or Mark again. Mark's "stay" with my folk's lasted over twenty years.

It was a wet Saturday. I bounced around the living room "dancing" alternated by pulling back the window blinds. Mother said to quit peeking out the window like a snoop. Eventually, dad drove up in his '39 Chevy with Mark in the front seat. My brother, an agreeable pre-teen, helped dad carry Mark up the several steps from the sidewalk to the front porch. The fascinating wheeled-chair thing followed along with a few bags of belongings. Mark was no longer settled in his chair when I rushed over and flung my arms around him and gave him a big kiss on the cheek. This impulse sparked a shock that erupted in a clumsy, momentary silence. Despite this, my mother fussed about getting him settled and setting out, I am sure, the ground rules. Mark was no exception; everyone had ground rules at our house as far as my mother was concerned.

Within a very short time, my mother cornered me in the hallway and promptly explained that there would be no more kissing. "We don't know how clean he is. You wouldn't want to catch germs," was her reasoning. It wasn't a scolding but I took it seriously and rushed into the bathroom to wash my mouth.

Considering what a change having Mark around made in our family life, I think we (and I use this term liberally) handled it very well. Cleaning duties were delegated as usual. Laundry days were adjusted. My sister got to clean his room each week along with other Saturday chores. Mark's breakfast and lunch were made along with our own and he easily accommodated the morning schedule for our only bathroom since he was asleep during this time. He also had a wonderful machine that I had never seen "in person" before—a typewriter.

Besides the paralysis in his legs, Mark had a slightly deformed left arm and hand, so he had perfected a one-handed technique on the typewriter that intrigued me. Since my room was directly above his during those early weeks, I would sometimes hear him pecking away at the typewriter after I had gone to bed. Words were his world in books, the newspaper, crossword puzzles and the mail. Not that he received much personal mail. He played

Chess by mail and he entered lots of contests with self-addressed stamped envelopes enclosed. He didn't seem to mind reject slips. Postage stamps were one of his few luxuries. Consequently, he cornered the mailman on a regular basis, wheeling out onto our large front porch to collect deliveries. I am sure he was waiting for some word from his family, but this was rare, if ever.

I wasn't privy to the conversations that must have taken place when it became obvious that Mark was stranded at our house, but mother did give us an overview and asked what we thought about Mark staying longer or permanently. I liked Mark but I wasn't sure what this meant. He was good to us kids, intelligent, well-read and good company. He gave my family as much privacy as possible and preferred to take all his meals in his room. Despite my pestering him with questions, he said little about his family. He rarely talked about them or himself or his past. Instead, he followed scientific discoveries, new inventions, and all matter of current events. He became my folks' eyes and ears at home when they were at work and the Johnson-family "neighborhood watch" on our corner lot at East 11th and Vandalia.

In those days, options for Mark's care were quite narrow. He had spent several years in a hospital from age eighteen forward after he had been stricken, and even worse years later living in a tent in Eastern Washington, while his mother was still alive. For a man a bit older than my dad, it must have been awful to be bounced about from place to place for years. He was on no assistance programs due to his disability and had no money of his own. Even though I found him a nuisance when we couldn't do something because we had to take care of Mark, or he would tell mother that I had run off to play when I was supposed to be doing a chore, overall we got along. Years later, he told me that living with us was "heaven" on earth. Even though he and my mother had many "arguments" over some issues (his smoking, for example), he said she was his guardian angel. He defended her with loyalty and

would tolerate no complaints about mother—or anyone, for that matter.

When I saw my dad laying a foundation at the back of the house and a delivery of two-by-fours arrived, I knew Mark was going to stay. Apparently, my mother and Mark had reached an agreement. A room was built for him and a small patio was laid outside the back door so he could wheel in and out. The front door convenience for the mail was lost but the new location opened other opportunities. Soon, he knew the schedule of all the service people: oil deliveries, dry cleaner, and garbage man. All became Mark's friends to such an extent that one day we had a call from Wright's Dairy asking if the young milkman was still visiting with Mark. It seems his customers had called about delays in their service.

I bore the burden of Mark's intellectual pursuits. He was very interested in ancient civilizations and made certain I could spell "archaeology" so I could check out books at the library for him. With my new library card, I had a very grown-up discussion with the librarian on Fifth Street, and then carried home a stack of books the three miles to our house. It was almost more than I could manage— but he read them in no time and I had to take them back. How we could have used a Bookmobile in those days! Like many other services, now taken for granted, simple things like getting a haircut were major undertakings. Very few barbers cut hair in-home but my mother pursued every lead until she found one. Despite his disabilities, Mark was tidy and clean. Sometimes he laid on the aftershave a bit heavy, but he made every effort to be presentable in his "uniform" that always included a cardigan sweater and slippers.

Mark became one of the family to my cousins and other relatives. They made a point to stop by his room and included him in their conversations if he was nearby. One year at Christmas, everyone pitched in and bought Mark a new radio. He was delighted and particularly enjoyed the live repartee of Steve Allen's late-night shows, predicting that the talented Allen would one day become a star. Due to radio commercials, he took up some hobbies such as plaster-casting and painting of miniatures. He loved the game shows and entered contests. One evening we waited anxiously by our telephone because Mark had figured out an exciting "Name that Person" contest on radio that offered clues over a period of weeks. The answer was dancer/choreographer Martha Graham—whoever she was. He was right, but the phone didn't ring.

One day I came home from school to find a quiet young man visiting Mark. He was introduced as Tom, his younger brother. Tom stayed for dinner and visited Mark again the next day. In the meantime, Mark said that Tom wanted the typewriter back. Horrors! I didn't know it was a "loaner." I was learning to type and had dreams of writing my 4th- grade Manette newsletter with it, so I was quite upset at this news. Mother never spelled it out, but I think there was more to this visit than a typewriter. She arranged for Mark to "buy" the typewriter, and if I am guessing correctly, laid down some more ground rules—these were for Tom. Mark tried to keep in contact with this brother, but it was a hit-and-miss sort of thing.

Mark's dad had been a school teacher, so a love of learning was integral to his personality. Mark helped my brother with his homework and Monty benefited from having a personal tutor. This didn't keep Monty from the occasional prank at Mark's expense as he was ready prey for lively boys. With the help of my cousins, we also pulled fast maneuvers on him.

It wasn't easy for Mark to get anywhere and he spent part of each day in bed. We would wait until we were sure he was laying down, then feign a telephone call or some sort of "emergency." This was a particularly good ploy when he was in the bathroom. During our spying stage, he had to put paper in the key hole of his room (which he locked as a precaution). Things had to get rather awful before he would mention anything to mother. Then, we would get it! All of this was probably incidental to the endless hours of our home life with noisy guests, taffy pulls, teen parties and music practice. He tolerated them all.

By the time I was ten-years old, I ironed most of my family's clothes. It never seemed like much of a chore to me even though it took a couple of hours each week. Mark would ask me to let him know when the ironing board was going up, then he would tell me all manner of stories—*Robinson Crusoe, Man in the Iron Mask, Little House on the Prairie, 1001 Arabian Nights* and others. He told them from memory and could recite many parts almost verbatim. Sometime later, I realized I had the distinct advantage of knowing almost all the classic stories, but the disadvantage of never reading them for myself. Mark wasn't my tutor in a direct way, but he was a good listener and someone with whom I could bounce around ideas about homework, term papers and such. He often saw my report cards before my folks.

In our Manette neighborhood, we got to know some folks better than others. I attended Manette Grade School and knew most of the kids my age. Just the same, it embarrassed me if one of my classmates knew where I lived and thought Mark was my dad. Those were the self-conscious moments when I had to explain away Mark to new friends or a guy I dated. It never seemed easy. No other family I knew had a "Mark." How could they understand my family? All this was rooted in adolescent silliness, but it still felt funny. Eventually, we became allies. More than once, Mark got out of bed to let me in the back door after "curfew" had passed. He said it was preferable to my climbing up the oil barrel rack (along side his bedroom wall) and going in the window of my brother's empty room and the risk of falling after dark. Guess this balanced out the years of fear that Mark would set the house on fire since he smoked in bed from day-one.

As time went by he became more independent and the trust level rose. My mother bought him a hot plate so he could fix himself simple meals when we were gone or took a trip. He loved it. Mark also fed the cat and dog.

Mark followed all the important events in my family—my sister's marriage, my brother's entry into the Marine Corps and service in Korea. He taught my dad and I to play Chess after my brother left home and, eventually, had a television in his own room. The only time he drank any alcoholic beverage was at Christmas, usually one hot-buttered rum. He always remembered our birthdays. Despite all this, I can't remember his.

He moved with my folks in 1957 when they bought a new home in Skyline Acres. It was a nice house and he put up a brave front, but I know he liked Manette best. Things were better when my brother moved back home for a while. Years later, after I had married and moved to Anacortes, he made a point to tell me he missed me when I came to my folks' place to visit.

After my mother retired, my folks wanted to become "snow birds" and live in Arizona near my grandfather during the winter and come back to Bremerton in the summer. They arranged for Mark to move into a semi-independent living situation that was, for the most part, very good for him. For the first time in his life, he had his own home; a small house with wheelchair access. Some social services became available in the 1970's that made this possible. His landlady bought his groceries and fixed part of his meals. He seemed happy with a remote control for his television.

Mark was stubborn—most particularly regarding his medical care. The few times he had dental problems, he pulled his own teeth. After he was on his own, he refused to see a doctor even after he began having pains, choosing instead to take a glass or two of wine each day. Eventually, the amount of wine increased. He died in his sleep at age 62. My mother made his funeral arrangements.

Some years later, I was shopping with my husband. He mentioned that Mark's brother was standing in the check-out line across the way. I was flabbergasted. It wasn't Tom, but a duplicate, walking copy of Mark waiting to pay for groceries. "What do you mean? He looks like Mark, but how do you know it's his brother?"

"I have seen the last name on his account card at work."

You mean Mark has had a brother living in Bremerton all along who never once called, stopped by, or indicated in any way that he was related?

"Guess so. I thought you knew."

I didn't. Maybe my mother had known, but I didn't. I wanted to go over and give him a what-to. Brad restrained me. "It won't do any good. Mark is gone now." He was right.

Marcus Stevens was an exceptional man because he dealt with his disability and the insensitivity of others with kindness and warmth. He should have had a better life but he didn't. Instead, he shared his intellect, humor and love of learning, and offered others the ideas and enthusiasm for living that were not his to follow.

About 1948—Marcus "Mark" Stevens with cousin Margie's arm around him. It is the only photograph of Mark taken I have ever seen. It was taken on Christmas Eve, one of the few days he would wheel into the living room and join our family celebration, and maybe try a rum ball made by tea-totaling Grandmother Clark.

THE CAT WITH NINE NAMES

Early in his stay at our place, Mark tamed a feral cat that was taking shelter in a crawl space under our house. No ordinary cat—he was a stray cat who found us. To be more precise, he found the crawl space via the foundation under the house. Slowly and patiently Mark enticed the cat with food until it would, one day, sit on his lap.

Each year on the anniversary of finding the cat (because we never knew how old he was when he "adopted" us) Mark gave him another name. To get the full effect, the new name was tacked onto the last one and had to be remembered in succession. So the cat became known as Aloysius, Lucifer, Cackleberry, Ailanthus, Fangslasher, Bickenbothum, Phyllis, Junior, Johnson—an impressive listing for any cat, regardless of pedigree.

It was considered an honor to name Aloysius. Whoever was chosen (and it wasn't necessarily democratic) had to give the name thing a lot of consideration. It had to be memorable and while Mark would solicit opinions, he was the final authority and official recorder of the names.

In time, Mark tamed the feisty feral feline to a reasonably well-behaved one. He named him Aloysius. I had never heard of the name and certainly couldn't spell it. I later learned it was the Latinized version of Louis, Lewis, Luis, Luigi, or Ludwig—one or all. When he initially named him, I don't think Mark had hatched the multiple-name scheme, yet.

When the first "anniversary" of his arrival under our house rolled around, Mark reminded us and announced it was time to give the cat another name to mark the occasion. I voted for something nicer, but Mark said he was a devil of a cat, so "Lucifer" it was. He was right. Aloysius could be mean. He certainly didn't like being dressed up in my baby doll's yellow dress for his "birthday." I wore the scratch scars on my arms for some time after to prove it.

The next year, "Cackleberry" was my sister Jackie's contribution. She had collected unusual and funny names for some time and kept a list of her discoveries. We thought it was delightful. My best guess is that Cackleberry is an old synonym for hen's egg. Yet nothing, it seems, could ever match the funny name our mother told us about. Seems she had a classmate named Harold Bottom. His nickname was the source of many childish giggles but it was rejected by Mark.

"Ailanthus" was another one of Mark's donations. He found it somewhere. I now know that it's an Asian tree or shrub—also known as "tree of heaven." Perhaps this was a way to counter balance the Lucifer moniker.

The name "Fangslasher" certainly didn't come from a present definition—namely a weapon in one of the *Super Robot* video games. Maybe my brother was ahead of the times because it has all the finesse of Monty's input. My older siblings were probably getting tired of the cat-naming game by the time the next anniversary arrived. That was fine as I got my chance and added Bickenbothum into the funny name category. It wasn't a Harry Bottom, but still amusing.

In 1949, my brother joined the Marine Corps and got engaged as well. He bought his "engagement girl" a diamond before he shipped off to Korea. It seemed fitting that her name, "Phyllis" should be added to the illustrious list of cat names. There was some debate about rescinding it after she sent my brother a "Dear John" letter, but we figured that event was one of life's bumps. Certainly, the cat had had plenty.

The "Junior" and the "Johnson" were givens that made their way on to the list quite early. They helped polish the eclectic assortment with a bit of dignity; something this cat could have used at times. There was some speculation that the "Junior" was added because it was an endearing term bandied about when my sister Jackie was expecting her first "Junior" who, as it happened, was a girl. After the warnings that no one would remember a cat with that many names, many of our friends and relatives took up the challenge and kept up-to-date in the naming game. The cat became something of a celebrity.

I guess it is accurate to say that Aloysius probably had nine lives even though he was a scrappy cat that fought and lost frequently. While we bought the cat food and took him to the vet for stitches, he was more Mark's cat than ours. Mark considered it an accomplishment when Aloysius would jump onto his lap and purr without coaxing. It was a particularly deep wound from one of his multi-day forays that wouldn't heal that caused his death. He didn't see the vet until it was too late for whatever reason and money probably among them. I don't recall many people taking their cats to the vet for shots, vitamins, surgery, or exercise programs. We bought worm medicine and occasionally flea powder at the grocery story or Payless, and that was it.

Giving Aloysius a new name each year kept us interested in what mother called an old "alley cat." He outlasted my pampered cats, helped educate the dog, and never slept inside until his last years (a delicate situation when I kept a bunny on the back porch). He was a cat of some stature, as we never dared call him just plain Al.

1947—It was a blustery fall day when Jackie and I had our photograph taken at the Enetai Inn in Bremerton, so it's a wonder our hair styles appear reasonably tidy. Yet, when mother saw the proofs with my blouse collar askew in every one, Jackie was blamed for my untidy appearance, not the photographer. I thought Jackie looked wonderful in her Bremerton High School Girl's Glee Club sweater.

THAT WAS NOW, THIS IS THEN

Cradle role for preschoolers at the original **Manette Community Church** with Mrs. Kennedy was my introduction to fishing. Sitting in a row of our-size benches, we watched her use beautiful felt characters to illustrate Bible stories. She taught us about fishers of men—a concept both profound and simple. Arriving early one Sunday morning, I found her playing the pump organ in one of the basement rooms. I was transformed. She let me sit on the swivel stool and explained how the air was pumped into the bellows by the foot pedals.

While church attendance wasn't a regular thing for my folks, they supported our participation, often encouraging my sister to help get my brother and I get ready. I hope their sporadic turnout wasn't due to the shock of my innocent drawings. During one service, mother gave me paper and a pencil to keep me busy. Inspired by the blue sky and fluffy clouds behind the baptistery, I drew naked angels in ethereal splendor flying to heaven.

My sister Jackie was a devoted member who took her baptism seriously and was active in the youth group. Perhaps more than anyone else, she guided my spiritual development when I was young. She was surprised I didn't know *The Lord's Prayer* by heart at age four, so she made me kneel on the cold linoleum floor of our bedroom and recite it correctly, line for line, before I could get in bed. It was okay. I wanted to know about Jesus and her explanations were succinct. My faith journey was a bit bumpy at times, but I had a solid foundation at Manette Community with its American Baptist affiliation.

I enjoyed singing in the choir, helping Mrs. Ricks with Vacation Bible School, and involvement in the youth group. When the original church burned down, young people were encouraged to be part of the new building program. We put on dinners and held other fund-raising projects to supply the new combination gym/social hall with sporting equipment. The summers on Vashon Island where we attended Camp Burton added a degree of maturity to our social and spiritual life.

My Baptist foundation was perfected and fully realized when I embraced the sacraments of the Catholic Church in my twenties. Once again, I followed in my sister's spiritual footsteps.

Manette Grade School was a large, imposing two-story wooden building. The six traditional classrooms had two doors on one wall with an adjoining full-length cloakroom for lunch buckets, jackets and other stuff between. There was a principal's office, a teacher's room, and a full basement with a cafeteria, of sorts. Most of the grade-group photos were taken on its large front porch steps that led to the south side playground.

I got a spanking with a ruler on my first day of first grade because I didn't stop talking. My own children seemed to enjoy hearing about this episode—and how they might avoid similar situations. Still, I admired my teacher, Miss Lottie Bell. During bad weather when we had recess inside, she taught me how to knit and shared news of her family's plight in Poland during WWII.

During the various grades, we took field trips nearby. We would walk to places such as the post office, the fire station or the beach. Miss Early was a master Rice penmanship instructor and taught us cursive writing. She also taught Third Grade. Mrs. Spencer visited our class each week for vocal music. Besides an occasional film (*Heidi, Tale of Two Cities, Scrooge*), we also danced in district-wide *All Nations Day,* and were enthralled by *The Bird Man* who talked about birds and drew pastel posters of them at the same time. We were also introduced to the instrumental music program. I played clarinet.

As we progressed through the grades, marks for good citizenship might be rewarded with participation in the school safety patrol program sponsored by the Bremerton Police Department. Assistant Chief Art Morken was its undisputed cheerleader. He visited regularly to remind us that a successful year would yield a special prize. There were never enough bright yellow rain hats but that didn't matter. We took our job seriously and escorted younger children across neighborhood streets wearing yellow rain slickers and using the red and white "Stop" flags. The end of the year included a trip to *Play Land* in Tacoma, free tickets for the rides and all the hotdogs and buns we needed to feel queasy on the bus rides home.

Later the yellowish brick "new and improved" Manette Grade School was built in front of the original building—eliminating the sunny side of the playground. This meant we had to traipse to the Manette Playground about half a block away at noon recess. As we watched the construction, we felt fortunate to know our class would be in the new building when school reopened in the fall.

We didn't realize the hazards we'd encounter for the privilege of using this leaky building. It wasn't unusual to dodge rain buckets in our classroom as well as in the communal "cafetorium" on the lower level. Our band practices were in the cafetorium. Here, we would hear the occasional drip, drip, drip—a "rhythm section" provided by Mother Nature. The year we entered the Sixth Grade, the school district bussed all the eastside Sixth-graders to Manette. I was glad to be back in the old building and a part of this collection of same-age students. It made things interesting, especially when the big front porch and steps of the old school collapsed noisily under their weight as students went to the new school's cafetorium for lunch. Thankfully, what minor scrapes and bruises they came by were few.

The Manette Playground was developed from leftovers of World War II buildings, encampment and recreation areas. When the tennis court was resurfaced and the wading pool built, it didn't seem to take long before a full-fledge summer program of activities was available. Sitting at picnic tables under two established shade trees, we tried different crafts taught by the playground attendant. Here we learned how to play tetherball, skipping games and how to behave in the pool—no splashing while an attendant was looking. Energetic college-age helpers, including the beautiful Shirley, paired with more experienced adults. They quickly established the boundaries of involvement based on our age and abilities—a "swing set" philosophy.

The playground was strictly a nine-to-five operation that captivated most of my summer days. What happened in the evenings had less structure. Some neighborhood boys found they could climb over the top from the boy's bathroom into the center room and let others into the building. This equipment room became our *Manette Club* meeting place. Since it was secretly accessed, the meetings took on an air of secrecy, as well. Far from Roberts Rules of Order, we regaled each other with stories, gossip and songs. I pretended to sing favorite songs "in tongues," a gibberish I passed off as a beautiful new language with some dramatic effect. The center room was also the "office" for the playground attendant as well as storage for extra tennis nets and more. In my experience nothing was ever taken, yet I suspect things did disappear because eventually the architectural flaw was filled in with exterior plywood.

Manette in Winter and during the height of the 1949 snowstorm, the lights went out. I fixed tomato soup and toasted cheese sandwiches for dinner for my folks and the neighbors. No one complained, especially since they had to leave their cars somewhere in the commercial district of Manette and walk up the East 11th Street hill to reach this magnificent repast. Much to my mother's usual dismay, our "old fashion" kitchen still had an oil cook stove and space heater, so we were comfortable and had a warm meal.

During this time, I wrote in my diary that I was tired of the freezing winter weather and frozen snow that lasted and lasted. Most years, snow was the grand finale of winter and I couldn't get enough of the wonderful stuff. With an altitude only a few feet above sea level, snow accumulations were rare. The "blizzards" of 1942 and 1949 were exceptions. In '49, I made an igloo by packing snow into buckets and dumping it into crisscross stacks. Since I couldn't figure out how to make the roof stay, it was open to the elements.

My snow sculpture of Al Capp's comic character Ma of *Dog Patch* fame, complete with corncob pipe and snow buttons on her ample bosom, created a neighborhood stir and some gossip. It dominated our corner lot. Best of all, it lasted longer than the snow melt, but someone complained to mother about the "realistic cartoon figure" and I was told to destroy it. As an aside, I think my family thought it among my best snow creations because they complimented me on my *workmanship*. My fingers would freeze with these efforts under soggy wool mittens. Two pairs were not enough, as they didn't dry fast enough on our indoor clothesline.

With a major snow event, the city usually closed off streets; among them was Ironsides between East 16th to Upper Shore Drive. Without a sled of my own, I would friendly-up with those who had a sled to share. We also hitched rides on either the Anderson or Filion toboggans—a bumpy bottom experience. We trudged up Ironsides for another ride dodging other sleds and snowballs. Very briefly, one snowy interlude, I had a truck tire my dad had patched in a dozen places and filled with air. Due to its size, it was hard to "steer" with small feet and hands. It was even more difficult to stay on top, especially with friends along for the ride. Worse yet, it needed constant maintenance—an intolerable waste of snow time.

The Manette News

Manette was an instinctual, fascinating place in my childhood. I wondered why we didn't have a newspaper devoted to its colorful characters, noteworthy events, and newsy atmosphere. In the summer of 1949, I decided to correct this oversight. The *Manette News* was launched using Mark's loyal Royal. I had discovered carbon paper, an invention which should make multiple copies a breeze. Like a real reporter, I walked around Manette with a notepad jotting ideas and studying possible story angles. I solicited information from my friends at school and family members. The content and layout began to take shape. It would be a REAL newspaper. The trick was to mimic the column format of the daily *Bremerton Sun* so as to lend authenticity. Methodically, and with Mark wondering if he'd ever see his typewriter again, I typed up four pages of news, cartoons, social events and "advertisements" for the first edition. It was a laborious effort. Day by day, with the project taking up half of the kitchen table, my family complained about the mess and the noise ---tap by tap—but never once reminded me that I was chasing journalistic windmills.

Finally, when *The Manette News* was complete, I had just three copies. I also had tired arms and a tired butt. Those three copies were the first and last of my efforts to launch a newspaper. My family read

the newspaper with suppressed laughs and curiosity. Perhaps they learned something about our neighborhood? With so few copies, I was judicious in its distribution. Naturally, Fourth grade teacher Miss Elliott was a recipient. She accepted it with a wary eye and a smile—and, no doubt, her own built-in spell checker. It may have read like any 10-year old effort, but the result helped me stretch beyond *My Manette*.

Facing page
1947—Our house on East 11th Street and Vandalia with our 1939 Chevrolet parked in front. When WWII ended, my dad and brother went to McCune, Kansas to buy the car from my uncle Lloyd Tridle who owned Tridle Motors there. They visited dad's sister, Beulah Tridle, Uncle Lloyd and other relatives. My brother brought back a turtle in the trunk that he called "The Arkansas Traveler" because the turtle was often found a block or two away.

Above
1947—Cousins Carlyn Kay (left) and Konnie Jo (right) Higgin stand on either side of me. They were adopted by Uncle Bill when he married my Aunt Kay (Mary Katherine). Carlyn (now Carlyn Smueles) edited the first draft of this publication. Ahem, she doesn't know I've added this note.

Myrtle Johnson. our Kansas grandmother, lived with them for a time, so their place was a hub of "cousin capers" and the best Halloween treats around. Myrtle would bake gingerbread men and tell *Trick or Treaters* that they had to show her a trick BEFORE they got a treat. The resulting "entertainment" was impromptu and sometimes amazing.

Top center
1945—Pals Chloe and Janet in back; (front l-r) Cousin Margie, Barbara Bowers and me in front, obviously excited or up to no good—notice the grip on the romper pants.

Right top
1948—My brother Monty on the beach at age 15.

1946—Standing between my cousins Margie Kay (left) and cousin Carlyn Kay (right) on corner of East 11th Street and Nipsic Avenue.

Above— My 1949 "Earthquake" report, first page.

Over lunch fifty years later, in 1999, Margaret Elliot, our Fourth Grade teacher, returned her copy of my *Manette News* to me (see page 54). She also returned the *Earthquake* report I wrote for her class that year. She smiled and said that at that time, she didn't want to explain how the sentence, "my sister raped her head with a towel" was incorrect (Jackie was washing her hair when the quake occurred). She also wondered how she might explain to my folks that the word "raping" wasn't part of our vocabulary list that week.

Eighteen of the 35 students in my Fourth Grade Class are shown here (top l-r) Clayton, Myra, Marilyn, Sherri, Evelyn, Barbara, Ruth, Paul, Jack, Mickey, Sandra, Marcia, Scott, Carol, Marshall, Carla Rae, Bob and Judith.

Miss Margaret Elliot

1947—A *Bremerton Sun* newspaper clipping about a Halloween Party—typical journalism coverage of news on the local "society page" in those days.

Above—One of the treasured Merit Certificates awarded to school safety patrollers at the all-schools assembly at Coontz Junior High Auditorium each year (this from the 1948-49 school year).

I didn't notice when my name was announced by Assistant Chief of Police Art Morken because he called "patrolman dean-na" to the stage at Coontz Auditorium.

He must have meant this for someone else.

Above—1949 with my folks at Thanksgiving time. Hum...where's the dog?

Below—1948 My grades would have been better if I had spent less time sketching in class.

Made in the USA
Charleston, SC
29 September 2014